GARDENING
FOR CONTAINERS &
WINDOW BOXES

GARDENING
FOR CONTAINERS &
WINDOW BOXES

EDITED BY SEAN CONNOLLY

CHARTWELL
BOOKS, INC.

A QUINTET BOOK

Published by Chartwell Books
A Division of Book Sales, Inc.
PO Box 7100
Edison, New Jersey 08818–7100

This edition produced for sale in the U.S.A., its
territories and dependencies only.

ISBN 0–7858–0246–0

This book was designed and produced by
Quintet Publishing Limited
6 Blundell Street
London N7 9BH

Creative Director: Richard Dewing
Designers: Ian Hunt/Linda Henley
Project Editor: Claire Tennant-Scull
Additional illustrations: Valerie Price

Typeset in Great Britain by
Central Southern Typesetters, Eastbourne
Manufactured in Singapore by C H Colour
Printed in Singapore by
Star Standard Industries (Pte) Ltd.

The material in this publication previously
appeared in The Complete Book of Container
Gardening, Container Gardening and
The Window Box Book.

CONTENTS

INTRODUCTION 6

INTRODUCTION

Container gardening, despite being so very fashionable today, is almost as old as gardening itself. Plants have been grown in receptacles of all kinds by almost every culture for centuries, including those of ancient China, Egypt, Greece, and Rome.

One of the reasons it is so popular now is because it fits so well with the trend toward small gardens. But container gardening is not all to do with making the most out of limited space. Design-conscious people realize that, if chosen carefully, ornamental containers can very much help in garden design by creating mood or "atmosphere."

Tubs, baskets and window boxes overflowing with glorious mixtures of old-fashioned flowers will create a cottagey atmosphere in a town or country garden, and it is even possible to have a wildflower garden in containers which will in turn attract some fascinating wildlife. Hanging baskets planted with *Viola tricolor* (heartsease or wild pansy) make an attractive display in purple and yellow.

Formality can be created with Versailles tubs, now back in fashion, planted with topiary specimens (also highly fashionable) and other trained plants such as *Citrus* and *Laurus nobilis* (bay).

There is a wide range of containers available today, including traditional flower pots, both plain and ornamental. There are tubs in all shapes, sizes, and designs, and these are probably among the most useful for the container gardener. Traditional wooden tubs and barrels, vases and narrow-necked urns in classical styles, shallow bowls, and long troughs are all suitable. And window boxes, wall pots, and hanging baskets are good for filling vertical space. Then there are novelty containers such as old chimney flues and wooden wheelbarrows. The most revolutionary container to appear in recent years is the growing bag, primarily designed for vegetable culture. What you use as containers for growing plants is limited almost only by your imagination.

🌿 **BELOW** *Almost anything can be used as a plant container. An old metal bucket is filled with pelargoniums and ivy, two favourites for containers. The container would have to be wintered in a frost-free greenhouse.*

🌿 **RIGHT** *Anyone with a warm climate or conservatory for plants like these – the large-leaved plant is Musa (banana); the big pink trumpets belong to Datura – can create a "tropical oasis." Of course they must be sheltered from frost.*

Containers should be chosen with care to ensure that they match the surroundings and fit in gracefully with the overall garden design. For instance, traditional or classical styles may look out of place in a contemporary setting and, conversely, the clean, uncluttered lines of many modern containers would not fit easily into a period garden.

Containers can be used for growing plants in various parts of the garden. The most obvious place is the patio, but any other hard area could be suitable, too. Walls of the house, garage, and other outbuildings can be adorned with window boxes, hanging baskets, and the like, while lightweight containers of all kinds provide the ideal means of growing plants on balconies and roof gardens.

In many climates it is possible to obtain color and interest all year round with carefully planned plantings.

The range of plants that can be grown in containers is wide, from small trees, through climbers, to shrubs, hardy perennials, bedding plants, and even aquatics. Many fruits and vegetables, too, can be grown in large pots, tubs, and barrels.

Container gardening has many attributes. It is ideal where space is very limited and can turn a patio, balcony, sunny porch, drive, or rooftop into a vibrant, colorful growing space. Even if growing room is not an issue, a container can make it possible to grow plants not suited to the existing garden soil, for instance, making space for acid-loving rhododendrons that will not thrive in limy soils.

Sadly few of today's small gardens have space for a vegetable plot, but vegetables can be grown in containers on a patio. Try "Tumbler" tomato, or like yellow zucchini (*Cucurbita*) and red-stemmed rhubarb chard (*Beta*). Growing bags, suitably disguised with pots of summer bedding plants, are ideal for vegetables but herbs, which are currently enjoying great popularity, are very attractive when planted in "warm" terra-cotta containers, particularly if the more colorful varieties are chosen.

Of course, container gardening is not without its problems: frequent watering is a must in warm weather and regular feeding is necessary in spring and summer. Potting soil should be replaced regularly, and container plants are most susceptible to freezing during very cold weather. But for most people the pleasure that is to be gained from growing plants in containers far outweighs the problems.

ABOVE *A classic combination—zonal pelargoniums (geraniums), petunias and trailing blue lobelia in an equally classic painted wooden tub.*

CHAPTER ONE

CONTAINERS ON THE GROUND

Most gardens are not complete without colorful displays grown in ground-based containers. Plants grown in pots, tubs, and troughs add an immediate note of variety or contrast to larger displays in flower beds. Sometimes they become the focus in their own right. While seasonal plants are popular and obvious choices for these containers, perennials, shrubs, and trees provide effective and attractive alternatives. Container gardening is the ideal way to inject a note of the country into the confined space of a balcony or courtyard garden in the city. Good planning can overcome obstacles such as intense sun and wind in these exposed settings.

Choosing Containers

No matter how desirable the plants, or how inspired their arrangement, if they are in unattractive or unsuitable containers the effect will be disappointing. It is not necessary to spend a fortune on buying containers – you can make your own junk or scrap and still have a superb display (as the illustrations of alternative containers on pages 48–49 demonstrate) – but the containers do help to set the tone of the garden. They indicate whether it is a fun garden, or a serious one, a garden where plants are paramount or one where design and taste are the hallmark. Choosing the right containers to go with the right plants, in a suitable setting, is what makes a garden distinctive. Whether your taste is for subdued bamboos in oriental-style containers or brash annuals in simple plastic window boxes, choosing suitable containers is as important as selecting the plants.

LEFT *Patio containers can be arranged with a tall plant in the center to create height (here a New Zealand cabbage palm has been used), surrounded by shorter plants (such as pelargoniums), silver-leaved cineraria plus trailing kinds around the edge (for example, lobelia). Other tall plants that can be used include Indian shot and castor oil plant.*

The container will also affect how well plants grow. They will almost certainly do less well in one of very limited capacity, which will hold less compost and thus a smaller reservoir of nutrients, and will dry out more quickly than one with more generous proportions.

Container size is important, particularly its depth, to allow sufficient room for soil and plant roots and enough moss so that the soil does not dry out rapidly in warm weather. As a guide, a realistic minimum size for a patio tub is 12in (30cm) in both diameter and depth. In a container of this size you will be able to plant several bedding plants or a single small shrub. However, more effective bedding-plant designs can be created in tubs with both a diameter and a depth of 18–24in (45–60cm). Something in this range would hold a larger shrub, conifer, climber, or small tree.

Tubs, pots, troughs, and urns generally hold a generous amount of compost, and the skill comes in choosing a container and plant that are well balanced and look right together (see the selection on pages 18–19). Beware of containers that slope inward at the top if planting trees or shrubs that will require moving to a larger pot in time as it may be difficult to remove them without damaging the roots or breaking the container.

The majority of containers are made from various plastics or from terra cotta, but other materials are used and they all have their merits and their drawbacks. Occasionally, different and very striking containers can be found, such as window boxes with steel frames into which can be slid ceramic tiles of your choice and, if you can afford to consider antique or replicas of antique containers, you may even find metals like lead used.

Fiberglass (sometimes referring to the patented brand name) offers real scope for the imagination. One of the most effective off-the-shelf finishes is imitation lead. Although expensive there are some excellent and elegant window boxes ideal for a period setting, and they are usually large enough to give even small shrubs plenty of room.

Glass-reinforced cement looks rather like reconstituted stone, but it can be cast in thin sections, so they are generally more elegant. Cement is used to bind glass fibers, producing strength even in a thin profile. Containers made from glass-reinforced cement are usually too heavy for window sills, but they make impressive troughs.

Glazed ceramic containers greatly expand the options where terra-cotta pots leave off. They are particularly useful for invoking oriental or exotic images. Generally they are generous in proportions and usually suitable for one shrub or large plant, possibly with a little under-planting around the base. Use ceramic containers to bring a touch of color and decoration to the garden, but avoid garish plants that will detract from the pot itself. Always check that they are suitable for outdoors.

Plastic is popular because it is low-cost and easily molded. Most plastic containers will become brittle after a few years, and may then split or break, but the initial low cost is an obvious attraction. The main problem is color. Whites look too bright when new and grubby when dirty; green never looks really happy,

BELOW Long-lasting fiberglass is a long-lasting material that can be colored and molded to interesting shapes, sometimes not easily achieved with other materials. An inexpensive material, fiberglass can be made to look like lead. The shallow dish shape is ideal for low, compact plants like Hyacinthus (hyacinths).

despite being a "garden" color. Browns are generally the least obtrusive. Plastic decorative urns and planters can be carefully painted to make them look more "antiqued." Plastic is an ideal material for cheap liner boxes.

Recycled cellulose fiber containers will last a few seasons, but are cheap enough to be regarded as disposable. Although the usually brown peat-like color is unappealing it can be hidden if trailing plants are allowed to cascade over the sides. These are containers strictly for seasonal plants.

✌ **RIGHT** *Strong and classy glass-reinforced cement can be cast in a much thinner profile than concrete and reconstituted stone, and it is possible to produce a finely-textured and detailed finish. Troughs like this have a generous compost capacity and this one contains a mixture of dwarf conifers, Hebe and Hedera (ivy).*

✌ **LEFT** *Short-term but cheap and practical; recycled cellulose-fiber containers will only last one or two seasons, but they are a practical choice where a lot of containers are required and the flower display is more important than the container itself. To buy more permanent containers for this vibrant display of pansies would have been very expensive, but here the cost has been kept down without any loss of impact.*

If these containers do not become too waterlogged, they can often be used for a second season.

Although not an attractive material, it can be almost hidden if plenty of trailers are used around the edge. It is even possible to cut holes (V-shaped cuts are best) in the sides for plants.

RIGHT *Elegant and permanent reconstituted stone is often used for large vases and urns, or any large and decorative container where a high-quality finish with fine detailing is required. These vases are tastefully planted with pink Petunia and Pelargonium.*

Reconstituted stone, a mixture of finely crushed stone and cement, is heavy and quite expensive. It is invaluable, however, for those large, elegant urns and *jardinières* that would be prohibitively expensive in real stone.

Terra cotta has a timeless appeal that looks right in a garden of almost any period, as suitable for a modern house as for a classic garden on the grand scale. Ornate and large hand-thrown pieces are expensive, but plain large pots are not much more expensive than their plastic equivalents given that they will last for much longer with a little care. Terra cotta, being porous, ensures that roots do not become waterlogged, and the evaporation of water from the outside of the pot in hot weather helps to keep the roots inside relatively cool. In winter it offers more insulation than, say, plastic.

Timber is the obvious choice if making your own containers. Timber planters and window boxes can be bought, and although expensive they will last for many years if looked after. Stained or painted, they can be integrated and coordinated with the house in a way that is difficult with other materials.

MATCHING THE SETTING

Visit almost any garden center and you will find a large range of ornamental containers suitable for use on patios. They come in many styles, shapes, and sizes.

Unless you want a somewhat bizarre effect, it is generally sensible to choose modern styles for contemporary houses and gardens, and traditional styles for period settings. The containers should appear to be part of the overall garden design and not as though added as an afterthought.

CONTAINERS FOR MODERN SETTINGS

Generally containers in contemporary styles have clean simple lines, and these are ideally suited to modern settings.

Tubs in concrete or reconstituted stone are probably the most useful containers for growing plants on a patio. The rectangular shape of troughs, made from similar materials, provides relief from the usual round containers and allows for some different plant arrangements.

Back in the 1950s a concrete container of revolutionary design appeared on the market. This was the shallow bowl, which looked superb with the architecture of the time. This type of container is still available and still looks good with today's architecture. The problem with it is lack of depth. The shallow soil dries out quickly in warm weather, so frequent watering is needed. These bowls are best planted with summer bedding plants such as pelargoniums, petunias, and scarlet salvias, and with spring bedding like tulips and forget-me-nots. The brighter the colors, the better.

Concrete or reconstituted-stone containers are generally pale in color, so if you want more color from the containers themselves opt

❧ **BELOW** *Warm and sympathetic terra cotta is an ideal material for the garden. It has a timeless appeal that makes it look right whatever the style or period of the garden. Although some pots can be very ornate, and are focal points in their own right, here a fairly plain design has been chosen to let* Impatiens *(busy Lizzie) and* Pelargonium *take the stage.*

➤ **ABOVE AND RIGHT**
Troughs offer an alternative shape and are obtainable in various materials, including terra cotta, plastic, and concrete. This enables you to match containers with the design of your house and garden.

➤ **RIGHT** *A modern patio calls for containers in contemporary styles. Many, such as these large tubs, are made from concrete, and can, if desired, be hidden with trailing plants.*

for terra-cotta clay. This is the traditional material for making pots and is a lovely warm orange color. You can buy ordinary plain (undecorated) flower pots in terra cotta, and they come in a wide range of sizes, including diameters of 12, 18, and 24in (30, 45, and 60cm) and larger.

Buy frostproof pots; these do not flake or crack in extreme weather conditions.

You can also buy plastic pots in terra-cotta color, but these are more suitable for utility purposes than for ornamental use, and most people much prefer the real thing on the patio. Also, they are very light in weight and liable to be blown over if planted with a tall shrub or tree, especially if a light peat-based potting soil is used.

CHOOSING FOR PERIOD SETTINGS

Readily available are terra-cotta clay pots. Some are very ornate classical styles, decorated with swags, fruits, and the like. These look superb in period settings yet do not look out of place in modern gardens. For a striking summer display plant them with red pelargoniums and violet heliotrope.

Containers are very
good for creating focal
points in garden design.
TOP LEFT Tuberous
begonias in a warm terra-
cotta bowl in a classical
style. **LEFT** Stone
containers come in many
styles and sizes. This
cistern-like one is planted
with pink verbena and
gray Helichrysum
petiolatum. **ABOVE**
Pedestal-mounted bowls
help to create height on a
patio and come in
traditional and modern
styles.

RIGHT *This*
attractively weathered
terracotta jar has the
advantage of depth but
the disadvantage of a
small-diameter top.

IS IT FROSTPROOF?

It is essential that terra-cotta containers used outdoors should be frostproof, except in areas where the temperature seldom falls to freezing. Unless the clay has been well prepared and baked to a high temperature, the pot will crumble or split as the moisture absorbed by the terra cotta freezes and expands. Pottery made in warm climates or intended for indoor use may not have been fired to this high temperature – always receive an assurance from the seller that the pottery is frostproof.

Beware of "Ali Baba" pots, and others that curve inward at the top. Even if the terra cotta is frostproof, it may not be able to take the pressure from the expanding frozen compost that it contains. Either protect these pots from freezing conditions or use them for seasonal plants and empty the compost out at the end of autumn.

Classical-style, often highly ornate imitation-stone urns, vases, and jars are an excellent choice for period settings. Keep in mind, though, that urns have very narrow necks which make them difficult to plant. Indeed, you cannot really create planting designs in them. A specimen plant might be suitable, such as a New Zealand cabbage palm, with its fountain of grassy foliage. Or a trailing plant might be good, such as a variegated ivy.

RIGHT *Period*
settings call for containers
in classical styles, such as
this reconstituted-stone
trough.

LEFT *Bushy plants,
such as shrubby
cinquefoils (potentilla)
create a balanced design
when planted in a tall,
upright container on a
pedestal.*

Vases and jars generally have wider
openings and therefore lend themselves to
more adventurous planting.

Large, square wooden tubs, after the style
of those used in the formal gardens of
Versailles, are excellent for displays of
bedding, and there is no better container in
which to grow small trees and large shrubs or
conifers. Traditionally they are used for
orange trees, and they are moved under cover
in the winter for protection against frost.
These tubs, supported on short legs, are
generally painted white, although you might
prefer to paint them to match the house if you
want a coordinated effect.

There are also other sorts of containers
suitable for patios in period settings. For
instance, you might come across old stone
troughs, or perhaps lead cisterns. Things like
these might come into the realms of collectors'
items – antiques which command a very high
price. But if you want to spend the money it is
worth bearing in mind that such items steadily
increase in value over the years and can prove
to be a good investment.

These containers are usually very deep, so
they can be densely planted. Sometimes it is
possible to buy replicas of old stone troughs or
cisterns which, of course, are much more
affordable.

TUBS AND TROUGHS, POTS AND PLANTERS

Even the best garden center or store can only stock a limited range of containers; it is always worth shopping around before buying, and it may be necessary to send away for some of the more specialist types. It is worth looking at the advertisements in gardening magazines; the more expensive reconstituted stone or reproduction fiberglass containers are likely to be advertised in magazines for the experienced gardener, or in "lifestyle" home-and-garden magazines.

The containers illustrated here are a cross-section of those available. Not all of them will be obtainable everywhere, but it is usually possible to obtain something similar.

1 French urn *This is a facsimile of a Renaissance bell-shaped urn. The plants should be colorful without detracting from the beauty of the classic urn shape.*

2 Reconstituted stone trough *This Adam style trough holds a lot of compost and is able to support a permanent planting of dwarf shrubs.*

3 Italian style jardinière *Reconstituted stone enables the fine detail to be achieved in classic designs like this Corredo jardinière.*

4 Stone sink *Ideal for alpines, genuine old stone sinks are now difficult and expensive to obtain.*

5 Terra-cotta terrace pot *A practical shape for many patio trees and shrubs. These pots come in a range of sizes.*

6 Herb or strawberry pot *These terra-cotta or glazed pots are available in a range of sizes. If used for perennial herbs the roots will become entangled and compacted within the pot and removing them from the pockets can be very difficult. They are great for small bulbs in spring and for bedding plants in summer, as well as herbs and strawberries.*

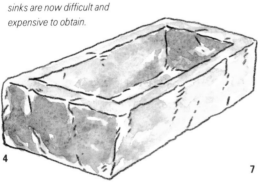

7 Terra-cotta ring handle terrace pot *The drawback of this type of terrace pot is that the narrow neck makes repotting difficult and if the compost freezes it could crack the container.*

8 Round terra-cotta pot *Round pots like these are very useful for bringing variety to the patio.*

9 Internally glazed Ali Baba pot *This type of container gives a Mediterranean feel to a garden.*

10 Pedestal and bowl *Available in terra-cotta or glazed, this is a good choice for tender plants as you can take it indoors for the winter (it comes in two sections so it is easy to move) where it will still look elegant.*

11 Textured plastic container *Plastic containers are very much lighter to move around than real stone or concrete. The range illustrated has holes fitted with drainage plugs so that they can be used indoors – just remove the plug to use them outside.*

12 Tower pots *Plastic tower pots are a good way to grow strawberries, as it keeps them off the ground, but they can be used for bedding plants too.*

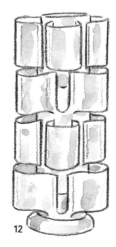

13 Oriental glazed pot *If fired to a high enough temperature these pots will be frostproof, but in the winter raise them slightly off the ground.*

14 Versailles tub *Elegant and classic outline, Versailles tubs also hold plenty of compost. They are one of the best containers for trees and fairly large shrubs. Although traditional timber ones are still available less expensive plastic versions are made.*

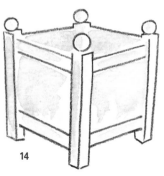

15 Barrel *Because of the proportions and depth of compost, barrels (or more usually half-barrels) are particularly attractive (leave them natural or paint them white, perhaps with black hoops), but plastic simulated wood barrels are also available.*

16 Ornamental tub *The harmonious lines and geometric patterns of many ornamental tubs are ideal for formal displays or for featuring a showpiece shrub or small tree. Take care that the display and pattern do not clash – simple displays are best.*

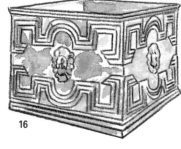

17 Recycled cellulose fiber planter *Useful for a seasonal display, choose plants that bush out well, and plant some trailers, then the flowers will dominate.*

18 Concrete container *Generally lacking in refinement, they are useful for trees and shrubs that require firm anchorage.*

19 Plastic shrub tub *Plain plastic shrub tubs are inexpensive yet very practical for a wide range of plants that need a generous amount of compost.*

RIGHT *An
imaginative use for an old
fireplace, it has been set
into a wall and contains
colorful bedding plants.*

FINDING ALTERNATIVE
CONTAINERS

For some people gardening is a way of
expressing their personality and creativity.
Making and adapting containers that are
unique or unusual can be part of that
expression. For those with a sense of fun, or
perhaps an inability to throw away something
that could be put to good use, and for those
who simply want to save on the sometimes
considerable cost of bought containers,
improvization has much to offer.

The ideas on these pages are suggestions to
whet the appetite; more can be found in the
pictures within the rest of the book. Part of the
pleasure of improvization, however, is
coming up with an original idea, putting
something unwanted to unexpected good use,
or modifying and improving upon an idea
already seen.

A word of caution is necessary. Except in
those few rare cases where a sense of fun or
mischief has influenced the whole garden,

LEFT *Half-barrels look
good in country gardens.
This one contains annual
helichrysum, an old-
fashioned everlasting
flower.*

unusual containers are easily overdone. A single surprising container discovered as you walk round an otherwise conventional garden will bring a smile or a touch of admiration; if there are too many or they are too vulgar, the effect can be off-putting.

Barrels or purpose-made wooden tubs that resemble barrels are widely available, but they lack the natural look and better proportions of a real old barrel. They are usually sold already sawn in half (occasionally lengthwise, but usually across the middle). If they are in good condition they will be waterproof enough to use as miniature pools, but they are really at their best as shrub tubs. Make at least three

holes about ¾in (18–20mm) diameter in the bottom with a brace and bit and char the inside with a blowtorch to help preserve it, if this has not been done already. If a wood preservative is used, choose one safe to plants, and avoid creosote.

Baskets of many kinds can be pressed into service. Large baskets such as old litter baskets of the size used in public places can look fantastic planted as a column of, say, fibrous-rooted begonias or impatiens. Line baskets with black polyethylene then fill with compost. Slit the polyethylene to plant the seedlings. Smaller baskets can be treated in a similar way but will require less compost.

🌢 **ABOVE** *Even old boots can be used as containers, particularly in country gardens. These contain mainly pink zonal pelargoniums (geraniums), with contrasting blue lobelia to make a richly coloured display.*

Boots and shoes will give a season or two of use in the garden after they have served their owner. But retain a bit of dignity – fashion shoes will look silly but old gardening boots, rubber boots, or perhaps even clogs, have the right image. Choose small plants that are not going to grow so large that they hide the container. Try a single boot, or a pair, near the front door (perhaps by a boot scraper), or make a shelf somewhere and have a whole row of them.

Buckets and bowls do not look elegant, but they can serve a season in the garden after they have been evicted from the kitchen. Drill some drainage holes in the bottom and plant very bold and bushy bedding plants, with plenty of trailers too. Then the plants and not the container will catch the eye.

Chimney pots, the earthenware pipes at the top of old chimneys, are always popular as "alternative" containers. Being made from clay, they always seem to blend naturally in a garden setting. Some are quite tall, so as it is only the top that is planted, pack the lower part with gravel or some other coarse material, topped with something like capillary matting to retain the compost and prevent its being washed away.

Demand exceeds supply, so some enterprising manufacturers are producing imitations. These pots are exceptionally tall but unfortunately have only a small diameter, roughly 6–9in (15–22cm), so planting designs for individual pots are out of the question. However, a very pleasing arrangement can be made by grouping several chimney pots together and planting different specimens in each. For instance, for a summer garden, some pots could contain trailing plants like petunias or lobelia, and other taller, more bushy subjects such as zonal pelargoniums or impatiens (busy Lizzie).

Growing bags, if available, are not particularly attractive, but once covered with busy and spreading annuals like petunia the bag itself is scarcely visible. Use new bags for vegetables, such as tomatoes, which require a high nutrient level, then use them the second year for flowers.

Paintpots provide a real opportunity to use colour. Make some drainage holes in the bottom, then paint the outside white to hide any printing on the tin. Once that is dry, paint brightly colored drips and splashes down the side (perhaps in red or yellow). Use compact upright plants, maybe in a matching color, like red tulips or yellow pansies.

Plastic kitchen containers should be used in moderation, but there is plenty of scope. Plastic bottles can have drainage holes drilled in the base and a "window" cut in the side about halfway up, into which you can plant, say, parsley or chives. Hang the bottle by its neck.

Tires can be stacked several high. Paint the outsides white, and plant in the top. This arrangement would take an enormous amount of compost to fill, much of which would be washed away as there is no base, so place a suitably sized bucket (with drainage holes) in the top and fill with with compost.

The bucket will not be noticed once the plants bush out.

If a tire with wheel is available, it can be cut and reversed to make an attractive urn-like planter. Drill a hole in the tire about three-quarters of the way up the tread to enable a hacksaw blade to be inserted. Cut right round the tire with the saw blade, then fold back the largest (the three-quarter part), so that the tread is on the inside of the "vase" (help may be required). Finally, paint it with an emulsion paint.

Wheelbarrows are popular for conversion. Metal or plastic barrows can be used, but for real impact the old-fashioned high-sided wooden gardener's barrow is difficult to beat – especially brightly painted, perhaps in red or green. Actually a wheelbarrow is quite a practical container since it is deepened to hold a good amount of soil. When the plants have finished flowering it can simply be wheeled away to a spare part of the garden, planted with other specimens for the next season, and then wheeled back into position as the new plants are coming into flower.

ADDING INTEREST AND STRUCTURE

Focal points are an essential part of good garden design. They give a garden a sense of purpose, and by acting as punctuation marks within the overall design, draw the eye to a particular view or angle. Such a point of interest may lure a visitor to admire it more closely, and view the garden from a particularly good position. It can also give purpose to other garden features: a path that has an ornament or seat at the end has more purpose than one that simply leads nowhere; an ornate container brimming over with bright flowers will lead the eye down a trained arch or an avenue of clipped hedges will encourage the visitor to explore. It can help to link various parts of the garden, and even create a sense of distance in a relatively small garden by drawing attention to an attractive view beyond.

🍃 **TOP** *A simple planting of* Impatiens *(busy Lizzie) and* Glechoma hederacea *"Variegata" (variegated ground ivy), made special by being planted in this old barrow.*

🍃 **ABOVE** *The juxtaposition of the large oriental-style container with the circular frame provided by the wall make this focal point doubly interesting.*

The plant here is Astelia chathamica *"Silver Spear", but a* Phormium *would work just as well. The large plant in the background on the other side of the wall is* Mahonia *"Charity".*

ABOVE Sometimes the container is much less important than the plant as a focal point. In this picture the pot is not decorative, but the plant immediately dominates the scene and catches the eye.

LEFT Containers do not have to be planted. If they are decorative enough in their own right let them make their own statement. These terra-cotta containers do everything a focal point is supposed to do.

Ornaments are widely used as focal points, distinctive plants can serve a similar purpose, but planted containers are also effective in the same way if chosen with care. The containers generally need to be bold, decorative, and distinctive. Often they need height, which can be provided by a pedestal, or a striking plant, such as a *Fatsia japonica*. Many reconstituted stone ornaments that are replicas of classic designs are ideal, but they should always reflect the style of garden. A large *jardinière* or a stone urn on a large pedestal could look incongruous in a small modern garden; a very modern-looking container in plastic could spoil the effect in an informal or period setting. Terra cotta is one of those fortunate materials that looks good almost anywhere.

In a small garden large containers may not look right, but it is possible to achieve impact by grouping together a cluster of smaller containers.

ACCENT PLANTS

The container may be less important as a focal point than the plant it contains. A plant with a strong visual presence can set the mood of an area. A single palm immediately suggests the exotic. Conifers, although more commonplace, are ideal accent plants by nature of their variety of shapes and colors. An unusual and distinctive plant, such as a cycad, *Yucca* or *Clianthus* will arrest the eye because none of these is commonplace.

BACKGROUNDS

To work, focal point containers should be clearly visible against their backgrounds. A dark hedge, or wooden fence, requires a light-colored container, such as reconstituted stone. Terra cotta and lead (imitation or genuine) require a light background, such as a wall of yellow bricks or pale stone, but more often it has to be created from plants such as gray-leaved shrubs or tall ornamental grasses.

The sky can be an effective background. On a sloping site it may be possible to position a large container in a prominent position, with a plant that creates a distinctive silhouette, such as a *Phormium* or a palm.

ACCENTS IN THE GARDEN

Use a pale-colored container on a pedestal, perhaps with cascading silvery-leaved foliage plants such as *Helichrysum petiolare*, and perhaps white marguerites (*Argyranthemum frutescens*, syn. *Chrysanthemum frutescens*), to break up a long, dark hedge. The hedge will make an ideal background and the planted container will bring to life an otherwise dull feature.

Flank a garden seat with two matching containers, and plant them with fragrant shrubs or scented annuals.

Provide a welcome by flanking the door with a pair of attractive containers filled with color and preferably fragrance. Use an outer container that is easy to replenish with fresh plants and be prepared to use plenty of short-term plants, such as reasonably tough houseplants like all-the-year-round *Chrysanthemums*, to keep these key containers bright all through the year.

Use a very colorful or ornate container at the end of a long path, to give a sense of direction and purpose. In a light position use a large, dramatic plant, such as a *Datura*. If the background is dark choose something pale and feathery or spiky, perhaps a yellow-variegated *Arundinaria* (bamboo), or yellow-flowered annuals.

Move in a container with a striking plant (perhaps a well-established clump of *Agapanthus* or a variegated *Phormium*) to enliven a border that has passed its best. If the container is very decorative you could stand it just in front of the border; if the pot is not a feature itself, place it within the border.

Steps are an ideal setting for container plants. The plants draw the eye to the steps and therefore help to create a focal point, yet they can trail down to soften a long or wide flight and use space that would otherwise be wasted. If the steps are too narrow to stand containers, it may be possible to use urns on a suitable support either side at the top of the steps.

Containers are invaluable in flat, formal areas of the garden, such as a herb garden or a parterre. Formal shrubs, such as clipped *Laurus nobilis* (bay) in wooden tubs or Versailles tubs, act as focal points.

PATIOS AND POTS

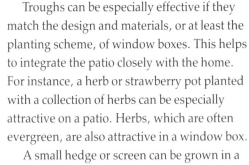

By their very nature patios are outdoor rooms in the truest sense of the word, and ornaments and containers provide ample opportunity to decorate them as one would the home. Being paved, they are ideal for grouping containers in an artistic and intimate way often difficult in other parts of the garden.

The intimate scale of a patio means that sink gardens and miniature water gardens are appropriate, and relatively small decorative glazed ceramic containers can be used more boldly without looking incongruous.

Troughs can be especially effective if they match the design and materials, or at least the planting scheme, of window boxes. This helps to integrate the patio closely with the home. For instance, a herb or strawberry pot planted with a collection of herbs can be especially attractive on a patio. Herbs, which are often evergreen, are also attractive in a window box.

A small hedge or screen can be grown in a trough. If several are used, each mounted on castors, they can be moved around to form a living screen to suit the day and the mood.

Some containers that may seem out of place in a more rugged setting, such as highly decorated and colorful bowls on pedestals, can work well on a patio. These containers can be used indoors or in a conservatory and help to link home and garden. Plant them with some of the tougher houseplants, perhaps trailing *Tradescantia* or *Zebrina*, to strengthen the link.

Because patios are usually in a sheltered position, or have a shelter or screen wall, they are good places to grow some of the more tender or exotic plants. A magnificent *Datura* in a big pot, a tender climber such as a *Bougainvillea* and perhaps a few tropical-looking plants like palms or *Agave*, will create an impression of warm climates and hot sunny days, and above all create an oasis for plants that like warmth and wind protection and which may not flourish elsewhere in the garden.

There is a natural temptation to fill patio beds with *Impatiens* (busy Lizzie), *Petunia* and other dependable flowering plants but instead why not create an exotic look? A raised bed of cacti and succulents can be a real eye-catcher and they don't require much care or maintenance. If the pots are plunged to the rim in the soil, and the surface covered with stone chippings or fine gravel, the effect is really striking. This works well within a patio setting but would look too contrived in other parts of the garden.

If traditional summer bedding plants are used, try to introduce a few tropical-looking foliage plants and this will give height to a bed or container. The large, often colorful foliage

BELOW *Dark decking requires a light or bright plant as a contrast, here provided by an attractive Japanese grass, Hakonechloa macra "Alboaurea" but other grasses could be used to good effect.*

will give the display more impact. Small *Abutilon* or perhaps a variegated × *Fatshedera lizei* are useful; *Canna* are superb plants, combining striking flowers with bold foliage. *Coleus* have beautiful leaf variegations and are easily grown from cuttings.

A water feature adds considerably to the appeal of a patio, and it does not have to be large to be effective. To achieve the sight and sound of water, a small wall-mounted gargoyle with a spout is sufficient. For details about pools and water displays, see "Working with Water" (pages 100–111).

KEEPING UP APPEARANCES

A patio will generally benefit from a combination of permanent plantings (perennials, shrubs, or small trees) in large containers, and a succession of seasonal plants in small pots, tubs and window boxes. This is one area where it is well worth plunging fresh plants in pots into existing containers as other plants pass their best, to keep everything looking fresh and interesting, at least during the summer.

GOING UPWARD

On the patio, climbers help to create a sense of enclosure and, as there are almost inevitably walls to be covered, they are functional too. Annual climbers in containers such as *Lathyrus* (sweet peas) and annual *Ipomoea* (morning glories) can clamber up a simple wigwam of canes or a small trellis; annual climbers can be used in window boxes if the windows are of the sash type, but are unsuitable for windows that open outwards.

Perennial climbers are better planted in the ground than in containers. Self-clingers such as the *Parthenocissus* will support themselves by clinging to a wall, but others like *Mandevilla* or *Allamanda cathartica* are best given an arch to grow over, or wire mesh or a wooden trellis fixed to a wall.

TABLE TALK

Patio furniture can seem bleak and boring when it is not actually being used. Keep a selection of small-sized containers – perhaps containing herbs or alpines – to group on the patio table when it is not in use.

ABOVE *Three of the ingredients for an interesting patio are plants in pots, a water feature, and a few tasteful ornaments, all of which are present here. Raising some of the containers off the ground helps to provide much-needed height and also masks the background.*

❧ **BELOW** *Paved patios
and courtyards can look
bleak unless plenty of
containers are used to add
character and height. In
this scene the use of pots
at a higher level as well as
on the ground helps to
make the scene more
cozy and "clothed".*

AN ELEMENT OF SURPRISE

A garden that is predictable is usually boring.
Even a small garden requires a few little
surprises. In a plant expert's garden it could
be an eccentric choice of plant – perhaps a
container with insectivorous plants, or an
interesting shrub such as *Corylus avellana*
"Contorta" (contorted willow). In other
gardens the surprise might be the container
itself.

In a patio garden packed with containers, a
couple of large terra-cotta tubs or bowls with
smiling faces, one perhaps winking
knowingly at the other, will immediately take
the eye and almost certainly raise a smile.

Paint pots (painted white, with drips and
runs in bright colors) can have a similar impact
and are more readily available. Many large
paint pots are now made of plastic, and these
are less likely to leave a rust mark on your
patio than a conventional metal pot.

Conventional containers, or even
earthenware jars from the kitchen, can be on
their sides, perhaps partly submerged in the
ground, with plants tumbling out as though
spilling over the ground. In a gravel garden a
single trailing plant set in the container with
the top growth allowed to run out over the
ground may be effective. In a position where
plants can be set in the soil as well as the
container, a "river" of, say, small yellow or
gold violas could be planted in the container
and in a spreading pool of color in the
ground.

An upright container nestling among
plants in a border, perhaps with trailers such
as small-leaved *Hedera* (ivies) tumbling down
the sides to mingle with the border plants, can
also provide an element of surprise.

It is worth having a few small plants in
ordinary kitchen cups, soup bowls or even an
old teapot without its lid, which can be set on
the patio table when you entertain. As these
containers will have no drainage holes, the
plants must be watered very carefully and
kept out of the rain, otherwise they will
become waterlogged and the plants will die.

Drainage holes can be made easily in
plastic containers, but old kitchen basins and
the like need to be used with care if they are
not to lower the tone of the garden (a bright
red kitchen basin put by the clothesline can
work, because it is in context, elsewhere it
could look cheap).

Small animal containers, such as those in
the shape of frogs, pigs, or cats, are worth
trying to tuck into unexpected places, perhaps
almost hidden by other plants, until suddenly
"discovered."

An old gardening boot planted-up by the
door can look both tasteful and amusing.
Surprise containers should be set in context,
positioned so that they are encountered
unexpectedly, or be really bold.

HOW TO PLANT UP TUBS, POTS, AND URNS

The planting schemes in this book provide plenty of ideas for grouping particular plants, although these may need to be modified according to what is available and the size of the plants. Most of the mixed planting schemes assume starting with small or moderately sized plants. Larger specimens are sometimes available, often with a rootball perhaps 10in (25cm) or so across, but it may be impossible to follow a particular scheme for a moderately sized container with plants of this size. Larger specimens are often best grown in a container on their own, or perhaps with an underplanting of low-growing seasonal plants such as dwarf spring bulbs or impatiens in summer, or with small-leaved ivies to trail over the edge. Do not remove a large part of the rootball in order to cram more plants into a container than is strictly necessary – either choose a larger container or use fewer plants.

PREPARING TO PLANT

With the exception of miniature water gardens, all containers must have adequate holes for drainage. A layer of coarse material at the bottom will ensure that water does not stand and stagnate, and prevent the compost being washed through.

Traditionally broken crocks (pieces of old clay flowerpots) were used for the drainage layer, but in these days of predominantly plastic pots this is seldom practical. Pieces of broken polystyrene tiles are convenient for covering the actual holes, and half an inch or so of coarse gravel on top will ensure good drainage. Peat can be used instead of gravel if very good drainage is not particularly important.

It is always tempting to use garden soil for large containers, but permanent plants in containers usually have to cope with less than ideal levels of moisture and nutrients so they should be given every opportunity to thrive. Garden soil in some cases will be a handicap. It may be unsuitable for the plants you want to grow – in an area with alkaline soil

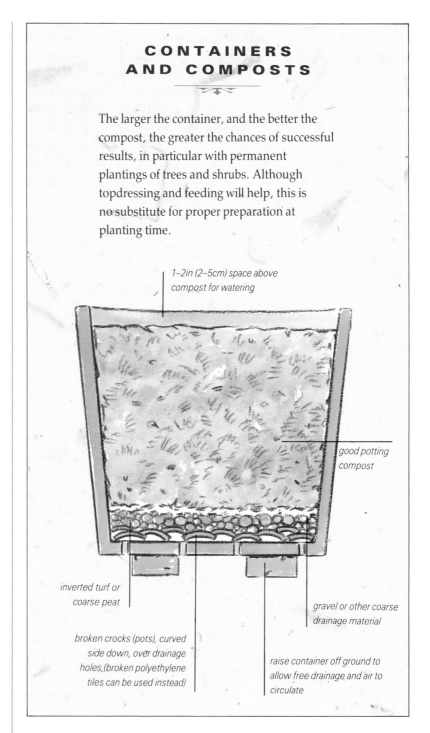

CONTAINERS AND COMPOSTS

The larger the container, and the better the compost, the greater the chances of successful results, in particular with permanent plantings of trees and shrubs. Although topdressing and feeding will help, this is no substitute for proper preparation at planting time.

1–2in (2–5cm) space above compost for watering

good potting compost

inverted turf or coarse peat

broken crocks (pots), curved side down, over drainage holes (broken polyethylene tiles can be used instead)

gravel or other coarse drainage material

raise container off ground to allow free drainage and air to circulate

Rhododendron, azaleas, and *Camellia*, for example, will remain sickly and second-rate if planted in garden soil; given a special ericaceous or acid compost in the container they will flourish.

Compost advice can be found on pages 133–134, but if it is necessary to economize for large containers, use garden soil at the bottom and fresh potting compost for the top 12in (30cm).

🍂 **RIGHT** *The most successful permanent plantings have both height and depth. In this trough Aucuba japonica "Variegata" and a conifer have been used to provide height, while varieties of Hedera (ivies) take the eye downward. Chrysanthemums have been used to hold interest along the center with patches of color.*

🍂 **BELOW**

1 Use plants of contrasting shapes and colors. In this example a spiky Phormium, *green and cream variegated* Hebe, *and a silver-leaved* Helichrysum italicum *(curry plant) could be used. Arrange them on the surface first to make sure the arrangement works.*

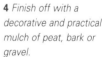

3 Repeat with the smaller plants in front.

4 Finish off with a decorative and practical mulch of peat, bark or gravel.

2 Remove enough compost to take the rootball easily, starting with the tallest plants at the back.

PLANTING A SINGLE SPECIMEN

Unless the container is small, it is best to fill and plant in its final position. Firm the compost lightly to about 1–2in (2.5–5cm) below the rim of the container. It may settle further with time, but most woody plants will benefit from a later topdressing. If the compost is very dry, water it thoroughly then wait a day before planting. Water plants in pots an hour or two before planting. Soak the roots of bare-root plants for an hour or two before planting.

Use a trowel to make a hole large enough to take the rootball. Most plants will have been grown and sold in pots, and adjusting the depth and width of the hole is best done while the plant is still in its pot. Plants in plastic pots can usually be removed by inverting and pulling them very gently; clay pots may have to be tapped lightly on the edge of a hard surface. Sometimes it is enough to lean them downward against this surface and to tap the bottom several times.

A few trees and shrubs, especially the less common ones that have to be ordered by mail, may arrive bare-root, in which case the hole should be large enough to spread the roots out as widely as possible and deep enough to bring the final compost level to the same height as it was when planted in the nursery – it is almost always possible to judge the planting depth by the soil mark on the stem.

Occasionally, some plants are supplied as balled plants – with the roots and ball of soil wrapped in hessian or a plastic substitute. Remove the wrapping carefully at the last minute, once the size of the hole has been checked.

Firm the compost gently around the roots before watering thoroughly. If a container-grown plant has been grown in a peat-based compost *make sure the compost in the container covers the surface of the rootball*, even if it means planting slightly deeper. This reduces the chance of the rootball drying out more quickly, especially if a loam-based compost is used for planting.

ARRANGING CONTAINERS

CONTAINERS ON THE GROUND

One of the least imaginative ways of using containers on a patio is to dot them around singly and haphazardly. Containers are far better grouped together, perhaps in groups of three or five, depending on the space available. This allows you to create some pleasing and coordinated designs.

For instance, a container or two at the back of a group could be planted with permanent evergreen or deciduous shrubs. In due season these would flower and be features in their own right. But they would also make excellent background for temporary plants, such as

BELOW *An old wash-stand has been filled with zonal pelargoniums (geraniums) and ivy, a novel idea for a tiny basement garden. The window sill contains a collection of scented-leaved pelargoniums.*

summer bedding plants, spring bedding plants, or bulbs. In effect, you can plan groups as you would in a mixed garden border.

You may wish to plan for specific seasons. For instance, a group for autumn might include a Japanese maple in a back container for autumn leaf color, while the containers in the front of the group might be planted with dwarf outdoor chrysanthemums and bedding

dahlias. A grouping for mild winters might include as background the evergreen shrubs *Mahonia japonica,* with fragrant yellow flowers, and white-flowered laurustinus; fill the front containers with winter-flowering pansies.

A spring group could have a deciduous magnolia as a background plant, such as the white star magnolia with its white starry flowers; or *M. soulangiana,* with its large goblet-shaped, purple-flushed blooms. Spring-flowering bulbs would go well with these magnolias, particularly grape hyacinths and polyanthus in blue shades.

For summer, try one of the evergreen escallonias as a background subject. These have flowers in shades of pink or red and bloom for a long period. The foliage makes a good backdrop for colourful summer bedding plants in colors which match the flowers of the escallonias, like red or pink pelargoniums, salvias, and impatiens.

Fruit trees grouped together are very decorative when in blossom and in fruit. A collection of dwarf evergreen conifers can also be attractive.

Sometimes a formal arrangement of containers is appropriate for a particular setting. For instance, twin slow-growing conifers of columnar habit, such as Lawson cypress variety "Ellwoodii,",Irish juniper, or Irish yew, could be placed on either side of a door in identical tubs, and through the years, carefully trimmed to the same shape. If the patio has a particular entrance, it could be flanked by twin conifers; so could steps which lead on to a patio. Here, place the tubs at the top of the steps. In a very formal situation identical plants are sometimes set in each of the four corners of the patio.

If conifers do not appeal to you for these situations, then consider formal clipped bushes of holly, box, or sweet bay. You could even have topiary specimens of these, such as mop-headed bays or hollies, or spirals of box. Topiary specimens can now be bought ready formed – but they are expensive.

Fruit trees can also be used in a similar way. Citrus fruits, such as oranges, look particularly effective in a formal setting.

RIGHT *Containers, including old chimney pots, are ideally grouped together rather than scattered around haphazardly. These are planted in a classic arrangement of upright bushy pelargoniums surrounded by trailing fuchsias and lobelia. Chimneys can also be planted with trailing and upright fuchsias and marguerites.*

BELOW *Single containers may create little impact when dotted at random around the patio, but grouped together they make a bold feature.*

LEFT *A popular idea today, especially with owners of modern houses, is to have designs in single colors, which are often coordinated with the house decor. This warm color theme is provided by pelargoniums, petunias and fuchsias. Other possibilities include marigolds, dahlias, and scarlet salvias.*

COLOR FROM SEASONAL PLANTS

Bedding plants, annuals, and bulbs that bloom in various seasons are among the most popular groups of plants for providing color in containers. Most of the suggestions in this chapter relate to seasonal plants – these pages highlight the role of color.

ARRANGING PLANTS

First, some general hints on arranging plants effectively in patio containers. With mixed plantings it is generally recommended that a tallish plant, or group of plants, be set in the center of the container to ensure height in the design. Surround this with shorter plants. Then, if space permits, even shorter subjects, or preferably trailers, can be planted around the edge. This arrangement is far more interesting than a perfectly flat design that is the result of using plants all of the same height.

Containers that are placed against walls should be arranged so that the tall plant, or group of tall plants, is at the back of the container and the shorter plants are in front.

COLOR DESIGNS

Color designs are very much the personal choice of the gardener. Some people like the traditional idea of mixed colors in their containers, while others will go for single colors, perhaps coordinating them with the house decor. For instance, pink designs are very popular and create a "warm" atmosphere. Red is a difficult color, as it can be overpowering if used to excess, but when carefully used as an accent color it can be very striking. For a sunny look choose yellows, perhaps with some whites, or with accents of orange. "Cooler" designs can be created with blue flowers, and green and white designs are extremely restful.

There are plenty of bedding plants in all of these colors. More and more single colors (as (as opposed to mixtures of colors) are becoming available among bedding plants, and this makes it easier to control colors and achieve well coordinated designs.

PLANTING

In mild climates spring bedding plants and spring-flowering bulbs are planted in mid-autumn, as soon as the summer or autumn display is over.

These are cleared out when they have completed their display in the spring. The plants are discarded as they start to deteriorate after the first season, even though some are perennial and may survive for a number of years. Bulbs can be temporarily

BELOW *A cool white and gray design for summer, using standard white daisy-flowered marguerites, with white petunias and gray-leaved* Helichrysum petiolatum *to balance the design.*

replanted in a spare piece of ground to complete their growth; if they are not allowed to grow until their leaves naturally wilt, they will not be strong enough to bloom the following year. Then they are lifted, dried off, and stored cool and dry under cover until planting time again.

Summer bedding plants and annuals are planted wherever there is room for them in late spring or early summer. All of those recommended here are frost-tender and would be damaged or killed if planted out before the last frost in spring.

Small evergreen shrubs are best planted in mid-spring or early autumn; at these times

they establish quickly. Evergreens can be planted on their own in containers; or they can share containers with spring or summer bedding – a popular combination among container gardeners. In either case, they should be considered permanent residents, as most will suffer from transplanting.

Changing seasonal designs is now easy, thanks to the availability at garden centers of ready-planted plastic modules, each containing a number of well-developed plants. These plants, modules and all, are simply placed in patio containers to create instant displays. You can buy plants that are coming into flower so that there is not the long, boring period between planting and flowering that sometimes occurs with traditional planting and which is particularly applicable to spring bedding.

Plants and bulbs are generally set close together in containers for optimum effect. They need some room to develop, though, so leave a little space around each. Arrange the plants so that the foliage is not quite touching.

Unless otherwise stated, all plants and bulbs should be grown in sunny positions.

 ABOVE *When changing seasonal designs in the traditional way, it is important to avoid disturbing any permanent residents. However, the introduction of ready-planted plastic modules, which are simply placed together in patio containers, has made seasonal changes quick and easy.*

SHRUBS, TREES, AND CLIMBERS

If you don't want to go to all the trouble of changing bedding plants several times a year as weather and blooming times change, you can use permanent plants instead. Many shrubs, small trees, climbers, roses, and hardy perennials do well in patio containers. Many people prefer to use a potting soil that contains loam, peat, and sand for permanent plants, although peat-based soils are also good. However, peat-based soils are not dense enough to provide a strong anchor for large shrubs and small trees.

SHRUBS

The best times to plant evergreen shrubs are mid-spring and early autumn. Deciduous kinds may be planted in autumn or early spring. Bear in mind that many of the following will not withstand very severe winters (below 10°F/−12°C) in containers, unless protected in some way. The following list includes shrubs which are suitable for various climates and soils.

Japanese maple (Acer palmatum) – Many cultivars produce brilliant autumn leaf color. Others have red foliage in spring and summer. It is best in lime-free soil and in a sheltered position.

Barberry (Berberis × stenophylla) – This evergreen spiny shrub has deep yellow flowers in mid-spring. It makes a good background for a group of containers.

Box (Buxus sempervirens) – Suitable for shade, this evergreen has small leaves and is usually grown as a formal clipped specimen, including topiary.

Camellia – This evergreen shrub has handsome glossy foliage and pink, red, or white flowers in winter and spring. Use cultivars of C. *japonica* or C. × *williamsii*. It needs a lime-free soil and a position out of early morning sun. It is suitable for shade.

LEFT *The box* (Buxus sempervirens) *is an evergreen shrub suitable for shade and can be trained to a formal shape if desired.*

LEFT *Container-grown Japanese maple* (Acer palmatum). *It needs a sheltered position and lime-free soil.*

Elaeagnus pungens "Maculata" – Excellent as a background plant and very bright in winter, this evergreen has bright gold-splashed leaves.

Escallonia – There are many species and cultivars of these tender evergreen shrubs producing pink, red, or white flowers in summer. It is recommended only for mild climates.

Japanese spindle tree *(Euonymus japonicus)* – This evergreen has shiny green leaves. More attractive are the white or yellow variegated cultivars. It thrives in shade.

Japanese fatsia *(Fatsia japonica)* – An excellent "architectural" background plant with its large hand-shaped leaves, it needs wintering under glass in cold areas. It is suitable for shade.

Golden bells *(Forsythia x intermedia* "Lynwood") – The branches are completely covered with large, bright yellow flowers in early spring. It is excellent as a background for spring bulbs but is uninteresting for the rest of the year.

☙ ABOVE *Lawson cypress (*Chamaecyparis lawsoniana*) is suited to tub culture and may if desired be grown as a mop-headed standard. The tradition of flanking steps with standards is still popular.*

Lawson cypress *(Chamaecyparis lawsoniana)* – The conical cultivars "Ellwoodii" (gray-green) and "Ellwood's Gold" (tinged yellow) of this evergreen conifer are suitable for tubs.

Mexican orange blossom *(Choisya ternata)* – This is a tender evergreen that is best overwintered under glass in cold areas. There are white, highly fragrant flowers in spring and early summer.

Daphne odora "aureomarginata" – This small evergreen shrub has highly fragrant purple-pink flowers in winter and spring, and cream-edged leaves. It is best overwintered under glass in cold areas.

☙ ABOVE *Japanese fatsia (*Fatsia japonica*) is an excellent "architectural" background plant for sun or shade. Its exotic appearance contrasts dramatically with the rest of the garden.*

LEFT *Heathers are dwarf evergreen shrubs suitable for various seasons with flowers in shades of pink, red, purple, lilac, and white. They should be grown in lime-free soil. Trim lightly with shears after flowering to remove dead blooms. Heathers can be used as ground cover around trees or large shrubs provided they are not shaded.*

BELOW *A mop-headed standard privet is complemented by crocuses planted around the base. Shrubby veronicas or hebes are evergreen shrubs which flower in the summer and some have variegated foliage. They are recommended only for mild areas.*

Fuchsia magellanica – Normally cultivars are grown, with bell-shaped flowers mainly in scarlet and violet during the summer. This is a tender plant, so winter under glass in cold areas. It tolerates partial shade.

Heathers – These are dwarf evergreen shrubs suitable for various seasons, with flowers in various shades. Cultivars of *Calluna vulgaris* flower in summer or autumn. Some have colored foliage. For winter through to spring grow cultivars of *Erica herbacea (E carnea)* and *E x darleyensis.* Lime-free soil is needed – remember that heather thrives in the acid soil of its native Scottish Highlands.

Shrubby Veronica (Hebe) – This evergreen shrub has spikes of flowers in shades of blue, purple, red, or white in summer and early autumn. Many are tender and recommended only for mild areas.

Hydrangea macrophylla – Flowering in summer and autumn, the mop-headed cultivars have large globular heads of blooms, and the lacecap kinds have flat flower heads. They come in shades of red, pink, and blue, plus white. Give it moisture-retentive soil and full sun or partial shade.

English holly *(Ilex aquifolium)* – This prickly evergreen is best in its variegated cultivars such as "Argentea Marginata." It can be grown naturally or as formal clipped specimens. It is excellent for shade.

Juniper *(Juniperus)* – Many of these evergreen conifers are suitable for containers, such as Irish juniper (*J. communis* "Hibernica"), of dense columnar habit, and creeping juniper (*J. horizontalis)*, with cultivars that have a spreading prostrate or low habit. All are suitable for shade.

Sweet bay *(Laurus nobilis)* – This evergreen with aromatic foliage has a pyramidal habit but is normally clipped. It is only recommended for mild areas.

Mahonia japonica – This is an "architectural" shrub with large, evergreen, pinnate leaves.

Long trusses of fragrant yellow flowers are produced between late autumn and early spring. It thrives only in mild areas. Although it is suitable for partial shade this plant needs to be sheltered from cold winds. It associates beautifully with architecture and paving.

Magnolia – Two are suitable for containers: star magnolia (*M. stellata*), with white starry flowers on bare branches in early to mid-spring, and *M. x soulangiana* cultivars, with large goblet-shaped flowers in white, usually flushed purple, during mid spring before the leaves appear. The latter is best in lime-free soil.

Mountain pine *(Pinus mugo pumilio)* – This is a dwarf, bushy evergreen pine with a somewhat prostrate habit. The foliage is deep green. It is excellent for including in groups of heathers for contrast in shape and texture.

Rhododendron – Any dwarf rhododendron is suitable for growing in containers. Most flower in spring and come in a wide range of colors. Almost all are evergreen. Dwarf evergreen azaleas are also highly recommended, producing a mass of flowers in

mid- to late spring in various shades of pink and red, also white. All rhododendrons thrive in partial shade and must have lime-free soil.

Rhododendron yakushimanum is rather special, being considered by many people to be the most beautiful of the dwarf rhododendrons. A compact evergreen shrub, it has attractive deep green shiny foliage with brown undersides; the new leaves are silvery. Heads of white bell-shaped flowers from rose-pink buds are produced in late spring. Cultivars are also available with flowers in various colours. It is suitable for partial shade but must be grown in lime-free soil.

Irish yew (*Taxus baccata* "Fastigiata") – This popular evergreen conifer has an upright, columnar habit of growth and very deep green foliage. It is useful for creating a formal effect on patios. A pair would be ideal for "framing" a doorway. It is a suitable choice for a shady position.

Laurustinus (*Viburnum tinus*) – This extremely useful evergreen shrub produces heads of white flowers between late autumn and mid spring, so it is a natural choice for winter and spring groups on the patio. During summer the deep green foliage makes an excellent background for colorful summer bedding plants. There are several cultivars including "Lucidum," with larger leaves and flower heads. This blooms in the spring. "Variegatum" has cream-variegated foliage.

Yucca – The yuccas are "architectural" plants with sword-shaped leaves, and bold spikes of white or cream lily-like flowers in summer on established plants. They are ideal for creating an exotic touch on a patio, perhaps in association with phormiums and kniphofias (see the section "Hardy Perennials" later in this chapter). They also look good in association with brightly colored summer bedding plants such as pelargoniums. The yuccas revel in hot conditions. There are numerous species including the popular Adam's needle (*Y. gloriosa*). Dwarf yuccas include *Y. filamentosa*, which has white threads along the edges of the leaves.

SMALL TREES

Many people do not realize that several small trees adapt happily to life in containers. They are especially useful on the patio for creating additional height to plant groups, and most produce dappled shade which may be appreciated during hot weather.

For stability, small trees are best grown in soil that contains loam, peat, and sand. The weight of such soil will prevent the trees from being blown over during windy weather. Plant in autumn or early spring.

English hawthorn (*Crataegus laevigata, C. oxyacantha*) – This is a round-headed tree that flowers profusely in late spring. Normally cultivars are grown such as "Coccinea Plena" ("Paulii"), with double scarlet blossoms; "Plena," with double white blossoms; and "Rosea," with single bright pink blooms. All are tolerant of cold, exposed conditions.

Japanese crab (*Malus floribunda*) – This is a most attractive, very hardy tree with long branches that arch over. In mid- to late spring these are wreathed with white or palest pink blossoms from deep red buds. They are followed by small yellow and red fruits. When these fall they should be promptly swept up; otherwise they may get crushed and stain the paving.

Weeping willow-leaved pear (*Pyrus salicifolia* "Pendula") – This small weeping tree has narrow, willow-like, silvery leaves. As it becomes established cream-white flowers are produced, followed by brown, inedible fruits. However, the tree is essentially grown for its foliage, which makes a good background for brightly colored summer bedding plants such as orange pelargoniums.

False acacia (*Robinia pseudoacacia* "Frisia") – This is among the brightest of all small trees, associating particularly well with modern architecture and paving. Nothing is better for brightening up areas of dull concrete. The ferny leaves are deep yellow from spring to autumn. It tolerates hot, dry conditions and atmospheric pollution and so is ideally suited to towns and cities.

Kilmarnock willow *(Salix caprea "Pendula", S.C. "Kilmarnock")* – This is a small willow whose branches are pendulous yet stiffly held. It makes an excellent specimen plant for the patio. Gray then yellow catkins are produced from early to mid-spring. It is very hardy and adaptable.

Rowan or mountain ash *(Sorbus aucuparia "Fastigiata")* – This small, extremely hardy, wind-resistant tree has a narrow upright habit, so it takes up little space. It is no good for producing shade, though! It has deep green pinnate foliage and clusters of rich red berries in autumn. These will stain paving, so they should be carefully swept as soon as they fall. It makes an excellent focal point and could also form the centerpiece of a group of shrubs.

BELOW Clematis montana *is a vigorous spring-flowering species. Although not generally recommended for container growing, it will flourish in a very large pot or tub.*

CLIMBERS

Invariably there are walls adjacent to patios, perhaps to help provide shelter from cold winds, or maybe there is just a wall of the house. Such vertical space is often ideal for growing climbers.

Climbers are attractive plants in their own right, but they also make good backgrounds for other plants. The more vigorous kinds will not take too kindly to being restricted in patio containers. On the other hand, there are several of a more restrained habit that will settle down happily to life in a tub. As with small ornamental trees, climbers are best grown in potting soil consisting of loam, peat, and sand. They can be planted in autumn or early spring.

Virgin's bower *(Clematis)* – Some of these are extremely vigorous climbers and are not good for container growing. However, the large-flowererd garden hybrids are more restrained and take perfectly to containers. Most flower in summer. Choose from such well-known cultivars as "Jackmanii Superba," deep violet-purple; "Lasurstern," deep lavender blue; and "Nelly Moser," light mauve-pink with a red bar to each petal. Clematis like cool roots, so keep their bottoms shaded with, for example, dwarf shrubs. But they like their heads in the sun so don't plant in the shade. Clematis like alkaline soil. The large-flowered clematis make excellent companions for climbing roses; allow them to intertwine.

Ivy *(Hedera)* – These are evergreen climbers that make an excellent background for other plants. Some have comparatively large, bold leaves, such as Persian ivy (*Hedera colchia*) and Canary Island ivy (*H. canariensis*). They have plain green leaves, but there are variegated forms of each that are more widely grown. They are not recommended for areas subjected to hard winters. Tougher is English ivy (*H. helix*), of which there are many cultivars with both plain green, often deeply lobed and cut, and variegated foliage. Widely grown is the Irish ivy (*H. helis* "Hibernica"), with large, deep green lobed leaves.

Jasmine, jessamine (Jasminum) – There are two useful species for container growing. For winter color try *J. nudiflorum,* which bears bright yellow starry flowers on bare stems between late autumn and late winter. It is suitable for a shady wall. *J. officinale* is the common white jasmine that produces masses of highly fragrant flowers from early summer to early autumn. This makes an attractive companion for red or pink climbing roses. Both are reasonably hardy, withstanding moderately hard winters.

Early Dutch honeysuckle (Lonicera periclymenum "Belgica") – This climber is valued for its fragrant flowers that are heavily flushed with red-purple on the outside, eventually changing to yellow. These are produced in late spring and early summer but invariably there is a second flush at the end of summer. It tolerates partial shade.

European grape (Vitis vinifera "Purpurea") – This is an ornamental grape with claret-red young foliage that later turns deep purple. It looks lovely planted with red climbing roses.

🐌 **ABOVE** *The common white jasmine (Jasminum officinale) produces fragrant white flowers in summer and contrasts well with strongly colored plants such as these bright pink impatiens.*

HARDY PERENNIALS

These are often grouped with shrubs to create contrast in shape, texture, and color. Many perennials will not flower or grow well in containers, so they have to be chosen carefully. Those described here are known from experience to adapt readily to life in containers.

Hardy perennials are best grown in a well-drained soil containing loam, peat, and sand, but all-peat soils are also suitable. Best planting time is early spring. Remember that most perennials die down for the winter and then contribute nothing until next summer or perhaps late spring. The dead growth should be cut down to soil level in the autumn. If grown in their own containers they can then be moved to another part of the garden where they can be hidden from view until the next growing season.

African lily (Agapanthus orientalis) – This is a half-hardy evergreen perennial with strap-shaped leaves and heads of blue funnel-shaped flowers in summer. There are also white forms. It is on the tender side and except in areas with mild winters is best wintered in a frost-free greenhouse. It grows well in large tubs and looks particularly attractive in terracotta containers. Given regular feeds, plants can remain undisturbed for several years.

Lady's mantle (Alchemilla mollis) – This low-growing perennial is attractive in all its parts, with pale green lobed leaves and frothy yellowish green flowers throughout summer. It is often used as a contrast for other plants and associates particularly well with shrubs of all kinds.

Spurge (Euphorbia wulfenii) – This is an "architectural" plant that associates well with modern architecture and paving, as well as with shrubs of all kinds. It is evergreen with blue-green, lance-shaped leaves and in summer bears large heads of tiny flowers surrounded by conspicuous yellow-green bracts.

Helictotrichon sempervirens – This is an ornamental grass forming clumps of bluish foliage that contrasts superbly with many other perennials and shrubs, especially those with large, rounded leaves. Many other small ornamental grasses may also be grown in containers.

Helleborus argutifolius – Also known as *H. corsicus* and *H. lividus corsicus*, this is an evergreen perennial with attractive, three-lobed, light green, spiny leaves. In early to mid-spring it has heads of yellowish green, bowl-shaped flowers. An excellent "architectural" plant for partial shade, it is pleasing with spring-flowering shrubs.

Plantain lily *(Hosta)* – These days hostas are "essential" perennials for many situations, the large leaves in every shade of green, plus "blue,", gray, yellow, and variegated, contrasting superbly with shrubs and perennials. In summer these low-growing, very hardy plants produce spikes of small, lily-like flowers in shades of lilac, mauve, purple or white. There are many species and cultivars to choose from. They are superb for shady spots, needing constantly moist soil.

Torch lily, or red-hot poker *(Kniphofia caulescens)* – This is one of the most dramatic of the torch lilies, with broad, grassy, evergreen, gray-green foliage and in summer bold spikes of light red flowers. It must be wintered under glass except in very mild climates. It needs very well-drained soil and can be left undisturbed for years when grown in a tub.

Moneywort, or creeping jenny *(Lysimachia nummularia)* – This is a creeping evergreen perennial with rounded leaves and yellow, cup-shaped flowers in summer. The cultivar "Aurea" has yellow foliage. It is useful for trailing over the edges of containers and may be planted around shrubs. It is suited to moisture-retentive or dry soils and tolerates partial shade.

New Zealand flax *(Phormium tenax)* – This half-hardy evergreen perennial has long, upright, sword-shaped leaves, giving an exotic touch to a patio. There are numerous cultivars, including the bronze-purple "Purpureum" and green and yellow striped "Variegatum."

Many very colorful cultivars have been produced in New Zealand. In cold climates (below 20°f/−6°C) winter the plants in a cool greenhouse.

Rodgersia pinnata – This "architectural" perennial is grown mainly for its foliage, which looks good with modern architecture and paving. The large, hand-shaped leaves are dark green but may be flushed with bronze. However, the leaves are not the only attractive feature: plumes of pink flowers are produced in the summertime. This plant needs moist soil and partial shade, as well as shelter from the wind, if it is to achieve its full effect.

🍂 **BELOW** *Plantain lilies or hostas are dramatic foliage plants which contrast superbly with many shrubs (including hydrangeas) and perennials. In summer they produce lilac or white lily-like flowers. They are excellent for shady spots, needing constantly moist soil.*

🍂 **LEFT** *There are numerous cultivars of New Zealand flax (*Phormium tenax*) with bold sword-shaped leaves in various colors. This perennial is half-hardy and in cold climates will need wintering in a cool greenhouse.*

A CITY SETTING

Containers can be at their most effective on balconies and in backyard gardens. Growing plants in containers is often the *only* way to enjoy them in a very small area. Walls can dominate a small balcony or courtyard garden; basement apartments often have the additional handicap of concrete steps and a gloomy aspect. These conditions would deter many gardeners, yet some of the most dramatic container gardens have been created in response to this kind of challenge. By concentrating efforts in a small area the results can be particularly colorful and delightful. Watering and routine care is often easier when all the containers are close together and, without the demands on time from a larger garden they are often better cared for.

The key to successful container gardening in this situation is to use all available surfaces.

DECORATING WALLS

A few hanging baskets may be possible, but with restricted space they are likely to be an inconvenience. Arrangements in wall baskets and wall pots can be just as effective, provided they are large enough, and they make better use of available space. The other advantage of wall baskets and pots is that you can have many more of them. It is not practical to have more than a single row of hanging baskets, yet wall-mounted containers can be fixed in as many rows as you care to cram in; the only word of caution is to stagger them rather than have regimented rows.

A massed wall display with lots of containers needs to be planned with care. Too many of the same type, especially if wire half-baskets are used, can look unattractive "off-season." By choosing decorative terra-cotta containers it is possible to have dozens of them and all different. Choose interesting shapes and designs to create an arrangement of terra-cotta that looks good during the winter.

A large iron wall manger will add character to a bare wall and reproduction mangers are sometimes available. Because mangers have

🍃 **ABOVE** *In the warmest months lots of house- and greenhouse plants can be used to create an impression of luxuriant growth in the confined space of a roof garden.*

🍃 **ABOVE** *In a small courtyard it is perfectly acceptable to pack the plants in tightly. Plants in pots, like this Acer (maple), can be squeezed into a corner to avoid wasting space.*

widely spaced bars, line them with black polyethylene or fix small-mesh wire-netting to the inside and line the mangers with sphagnum moss.

Troughs positioned at the foot of a wall will enable a range of climbers to be grown. Self-clingers such as *Parthenocissus* may be too vigorous, but annual climbers or permanent wall shrubs, or perhaps large-flowered hybrid *Clematis* (generally less vigorous than many of the species), or hybrid *Bougainvillea* can be trained up a decorative wooden trellis fixed to the wall.

STEPS

Planted containers will soften the harsh outline of steps. Freestanding pots can be stood on the treads if space allows. A climber or wall shrub planted in a large tub at the base of the flight will break up an expanse of a brick or concrete wall in a courtyard.

BALCONIES

Lightweight containers are a sensible precaution for balconies. It is unwise to use heavy containers, such as concrete tubs, unless you are sure that the structure is capable of supporting them.

Plastic containers and peat-based composts are suitable for most plants you are likely to want to grow, but larger trees and shrubs will need a heavier loam-based compost and a substantial tub (perhaps a wooden half-barrel or a Versailles tub) to give stability in what can be an exposed and windy position.

A well-designed balcony garden should look good from the apartment and attractive from the ground. Containers at the edge of the balcony are useful for trailers, which can do much to soften the outline of the building.

Try using large plants, such as *Yucca* and *Monstera*, which can provide interesting foliage shapes.

SUN AND WIND

Being high up, balconies and roofs are often more prone to the effects of cold winds than lower levels. Wind can lash plants around and damage them. Drying winds can quickly dry out the soil and give the foliage windburn. Plants may also receive too much sun. Extremely hot sun may not only damage the plants themselves; it can also dry the soil.

If you know that sun or wind is going to be a problem, try to choose plants that will tolerate them.

PLANTS THAT
LIKE PLENTY OF SUN

With collections of both temporary bedding plants and permanent plants you can have color and interest all year round.

There are many permanent plants like shrubs that can be grown in tubs and that love hot, sunny conditions. Rock rose (*Cistus*) immediately springs to mind; it is a small, evergreen bushy plant that produces single rose-like blooms in pink or white during

summer. Many of these have pleasantly aromatic foliage, and the fragrance is brought out by hot sun so that your balcony or roof garden could end up smelling like Mediterranean maquis. Rock rose is only suited to mild climates, and will tolerate minimum temperatures of 23°F (−5°C).

The shrubby cinquefoils (*Potentillas*) also revel in the sun, and with their mainly yellow flowers make ideal companions for rock roses. They flower continuously all summer.

Lavenders can be grown with these for color and texture contrast. They have grayish, aromatic evergreen foliage, and blue flowers in summer.

Another gray-leaved everygreen shrub well worth growing with other plants, but only in mild climates, is *Senecio laxifolius*. The somewhat oval leaves are silvery-gray and covered with white felt on the undersides. Summer brings on bright yellow daisy flowers; some people dislike them and cut them off before they develop.

Some of the smaller olearias or daisy bushes are ideal for our purpose but are suited only to mild climates. The evergreen *O. x stellulata* has a rather sprawling habit and produces heads of white daisy flowers in late spring or early summer.

Escallonias are mild-climate evergreen shrubs, but where they can be grown they make a marvelous show of red, pink, or white flowers in early summer. The smaller-growing hybrids and cultivars are suitable for tubs.

Dwarf conifers would be ideal for sunny balconies and roof gardens. Provided the atmosphere is not polluted, dwarf pines would thrive. Try *Pinus sylvestris* "Beuvronensis," which is very hardy and makes a dome-shaped specimen. Equally hardy is the mountain pine (*Pinus mugo*) and its cultivars, which have very dense dark green foliage. All pines are evergreen.

There are many sun-loving alpines and dwarf perennials such as houseleeks (*Sempervivum*); sedums of all kinds; the red valerian (*Centranthus ruber*), with heads of small red, pink, or white blooms over a long period in summer and autumn; and a veritable

BELOW *Provided roofs are strong enough to take the weight, beautiful gardens can be created high above the city streets. Climbers and shrubs have been used to soften the walls to make a cool, well-screened area to sit in. Pelargoniums, impatiens and hydrangeas have been added for summer colour.*

galaxy of small silver- or gray-leaved plants like *Anthemis cupaniana,* with white daisy flowers in summer; *Artemisia schmidtiana* "Nana," which forms a neat mound of feathery silver-gray foliage: and for mild areas *Convolvulus cneorum,* with silky, silvery foliage and white, saucer-shaped flowers in summer and the curry plant (*Helichrysum angustifolium*) (it really does smell of curry), with narrow intensely silvery leaves and yellow flowers.

PLANTS THAT TOLERATE WIND

Some larger shrubs can be recommended to give height to a garden:

Bamboo *(Arundinaria japonica)* – Although only moderately hardy, this bamboo takes wind in its stride. The wind easily passes through its clump of olive green canes, rustling the long, lance-shaped, dark evergreen leaves.

Smoke bush *(Cotinus coggygria)* – This very hardy shrub is noted for its autumn leaf color, which comes in flame shades.

Silver berry *(Elaeagnus commutata)* – This extremely hardy shrub has intensely silver foliage and, in late spring, fragrant white flowers.

Kerria japonica "Variegata" – This shrub gives color and interest in spring and throughout summer. The deciduous foliage is variegated creamy white, and yellow flowers are produced in the spring. A pleasing picture is created when spring-flowering bulbs are planted around it, such as blue grape hyacinths (Muscari).

One might think that some of the tall ornamental grasses are highly unsuitable for windy situations, but in fact they are very wind-resistant; wind filters easily through the stems so that they do not flatten. All of these grasses associate particularly well with shrubs, providing dramatic contrast in leaf shape, texture, and color.

Zebra grass *(Miscanthus sinensis "Zebrinus")* – This plant grows to about 4ft (1.2m) in height, somewhat lower than the species that can

reach about 6ft (1.8m). The arching leaves of the cultivar are banded with yellow. It is a very hardy grass.

Amur silver grass *(Miscanthus saccariflorus)* – Often planted as a windbreak in gardens, this plant can grow up to 10ft (3m) in height. It has narrow, medium green leaves that arch over.

Gardener's garters *(Phalaris arundinacea "Picta")* – One way to contain this grass is to grow it in a tub. In gardens it is inclined to spread vigorously. But it is one of the most beautiful of the ornamental grasses, with its white and green striped foliage that rustles in the wind. This is a lower-growing grass at only 2ft (60cm) in height; it is very hardy.

Feather grass, or needlegrass *(Stipagigantea)* – This plant is not so hardy and therefore recommended only for areas where minimum temperatures are not below 10°F (−12°C). It can grow to about 6ft (1.8m) in height. The virtually evergreen foliage is grayish green and in summer bold, attractive silvery purple plumes of flowers are produced.

🍃 **ABOVE** *Good use has been made of vertical space in this roof garden by growing climbers up the walls. The perimeter railings make a home for wisteria and other climbers.*

TAKING THE
COUNTRY TO TOWN

A sense of fun and an apparent lack of organization are the hallmarks of the country garden. An atmosphere of a cottage garden on a warm summer's afternoon can easily be introduced to a small, town patio or country residence by way of a few simple planters, in fact the simpler the better. A hodgepodge of well-worn containers gives an ideal framework, while a soft style of planting completes the picture. Beyond these guidelines readers can experiment to their hearts' content. There is infinite scope but try to include some scented plants, and some varieties which will extend the display beyond the summer months.

🌿 **BELOW A summer barrel** *Ingredients for a 24in (60cm) barrel:*

1 Althaea rosea *(hollyhock)* x 3

2 *pink* Penstemon

3 *mixed* Nicotiana x 6

4 Alchemilla mollis *(lady's mantle)*

5 Fragaria *(strawberry)*

6 *pink* Diascia

7 Saxifraga stolonifera *"Tricolor"*

8 *blue-violet* Aster amellus *(Michaelmas daisy)*

9 Lilium auratum *"Apollo"* x 3

10 Foeniculum vulgare *(fennel).*

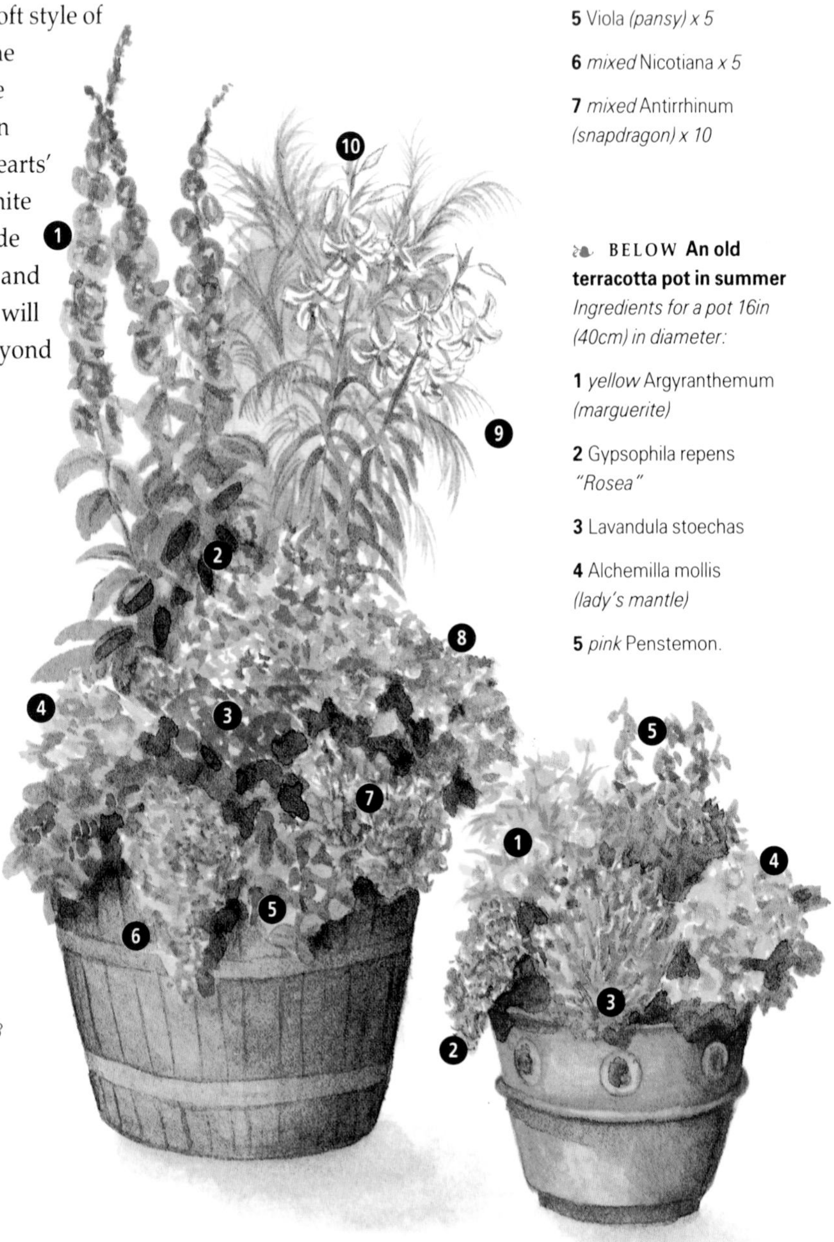

🌿 **RIGHT Window box with picket fence**
Ingredients for a window box 3ft (1m) long:

1 Amaranthus caudatus *x 3*

2 Alyssum *x 12*

3 Lathyrus *(sweet pea)* x 6

4 Tropaeolum majus *(nasturtium)* x 10

5 Viola *(pansy)* x 5

6 *mixed* Nicotiana x 5

7 *mixed* Antirrhinum *(snapdragon)* x 10

🌿 **BELOW An old terracotta pot in summer**
Ingredients for a pot 16in (40cm) in diameter:

1 *yellow* Argyranthemum *(marguerite)*

2 Gypsophila repens *"Rosea"*

3 Lavandula stoechas

4 Alchemilla mollis *(lady's mantle)*

5 *pink* Penstemon.

🌿 BELOW **A basket full of London pride** Saxifraga x urbium *(London pride) (direct). The contents can be changed for different potted plants as they come into flower.*

🌿 BOTTOM **Watering can** *Blue trailing* Lobelia *acts as a floral substitute for the usual contents.*

🌿 LEFT **An old chimney pot** *This provides a raised position from which* Convolvulus mauritanicus *cascades down.*

🌿 BOTTOM RIGHT **An old-style wooden wheelbarrow** *This makes a fine feature by a front door. Wooden barrels and other rustic containers play an important part in creating a country atmosphere. Ingredients:*

1 Tagetes tenuifolia *"Pumila" Starfire Mixed x 5*

2 Erigeron mucronatus *x 6*

3 *rich red* Petunia x 3

4 Convulvulus mauritanicus *x 2*

5 Tropaeolum majus *"Alaska" (nasturtium) x 6*

6 *variegated* Pelargonium

7 *red and purple* Fuchsia

CHAPTER TWO

WINDOW
BOXES

A dazzling display of flowers along the sill is the ultimate window dressing. Window boxes can transform unremarkable windows or draw attention to the finer architectural features of a period property. A colorful window box is the best advertisement for a gardener's skill or sense of individuality. But as in so much good gardening, special attention to plant height, blooming periods, and situation lies behind even the most spontaneous display.

LEFT *A riot of colors is appropriate for the traditional English cottage style of garden and needs a plain uncluttered background.*

Window boxes are an ideal way to garden. They are easy to install, simple to plant, and fun to care for. They do not require endless hours of digging, bending, and weeding to maintain. Best of all, window boxes make flowers and greenery a part of your home, growing in a place where you will see the plants often and derive continuous enjoyment from them. If you have never gardened before, planting a window box or two will enable you to try your hand at growing plants on a small and very manageable scale. If you already garden in the courtyard, or on a patio or rooftop, window boxes can add extra sparkle to your landscape.

Whether you live and garden in the city or country, window boxes can delight your eye and help decorate your home while demanding little of your time, money, or labor.

It probably comes as a surprise to learn that window boxes have been used for growing plants since Roman times – if not even earlier. These were undoubtedly earthenware containers, but since then many other materials have been used for making them. In the Middle Ages, for instance, window boxes were made from wattle or strips of wood woven together, as well as from metal, and again clay, especially terra cotta.

Gardening in window boxes is quite different from gardening in beds and borders. You will be able to exercise more control over the soil mix in which the plants grow. Plants in window boxes need to be watered and fertilized more frequently than plants in garden beds, because the volume of soil is so much smaller. It dries out rapidly and its nutrients become exhausted quickly. This chapter provides basic instructions on how to garden in window boxes.

CONTAINERS

A window box that will sit directly on the window sill should be a few inches shorter than the width of the sill so that you can get your hands around the ends of the box when you lift it on and off the sill. If you will be mounting the box on the wall below the window sill, the length is not as critical. The window box can be a bit wider than the window sill and supported with brackets screwed or bolted into the wall.

When choosing a container for your window box, get the deepest one you can find. It should be at least 6in (15cm) deep – 12in (30cm) is even better, if your window is large enough to accommodate it. The deeper the box, the more space is available for plant roots, and the wider your choice of plants. Also, since a deeper box holds more soil, the box will not dry out so rapidly.

Simple containers are the most versatile. A plain container blends in with most architectural styles, and does not detract attention from the plants growing inside it. Neutral colors – gray, beige, brown, natural wood – do not detract from the colors of the building or the plants. Window boxes are also available in white (which will need frequent cleaning, especially in dirty city air) or green. You can also paint the boxes to match the trim on your house. If you plan to mount the boxes on the wall below the window sills, you may want to paint them the same color as the wall. Keep in mind that flat matt paint does not stand out as much as glossy paint, and is probably a better choice for window boxes.

CHOOSING AND INSTALLING WINDOW BOXES

You can choose from a number of different materials when selecting window boxes. One of the best is fiberglass. Fiberglass boxes are durable, hold up well in both hot and cold weather, and are relatively inexpensive. They are also easy to clean – a real plus.

Terra cotta is still used, and these boxes look very nice, too, especially on older-style properties, including country houses. They often have ornate relief designs. But there is one drawback with terra-cotta window boxes. Being porous, the soil is inclined to dry out rapidly during warm weather.

In the past lead window boxes were popular, and today it is still possible to buy them in this material, generally in traditional styles, because these look most "comfortable" when installed in period homes. Although most lead window boxes are not large, they are expensive and, of course, very heavy.

Many window boxes today are made from plastic and come in various sizes, colors, and styles. Plastic is more suitable for modern settings and has the advantage of being lightweight and therefore easy to handle. Because plastic is nonporous, the soil in such boxes dries out less quickly than in, for example, terra-cotta boxes. If you opt for plastic boxes, make sure they are made of a durable, heavyweight plastic; cheap, thin plastic boxes become brittle after spending time in the sunlight, and tend to crack and break.

Wood is the classic material for window boxes. You can buy ready-made boxes or build your own, if you are so inclined. The natural look of stained or varnished wood is ideal for country houses and summer or weekend homes. Painted wood boxes can look sophisticated enough for a contemporary or city home. Wood is a good insulator, and protects plant roots from extreme temperatures better than plastic, clay, or metal boxes. Teak and redwood make especially durable containers.

Wooden window boxes are very popular today, due to a great extent to the many styles and finishes in which they are available. There are modern styles in wood to suit contemporary houses, traditional styles for traditional homes, and more rustic boxes for country houses.

The insides of wooden window boxes should be treated every two years with a horticultural wood preservative to prevent rotting. Never use a non-horticultural preservative; you could damage plants if you do. The outsides of boxes can be similarly treated if you want a natural wood finish. You could choose a colored wood preservative, such as dark oak or teak, or use a clear preservative. Alternatively, wooden window boxes can be painted on the outside to coordinate with the building.

Metal containers are less desirable because they rust quickly and are good conductors of heat and cold, and therefore do little to insulate plant roots from fluctuating temperatures. If you do choose metal boxes,

make sure they are well painted or coated with plastic or polyurethane to make them last as long as possible.

Terra-cotta window boxes are attractive and natural-looking and their neutral color complements many flower colors. Unglazed clay or terra-cotta window boxes are porous and allow moisture to transpire quickly through their sides. They also break easily, especially in cold weather. (Freezing temperatures often crack them.)

ABOVE *Window boxes can be integrated with both the home and the surrounding plants by choosing a sympathetic color that blends and using colors that harmonize. Trailing Glechoma hederacea (ground ivy) ties in with the vertical habit climbing Ipomoea (Morning glory).*

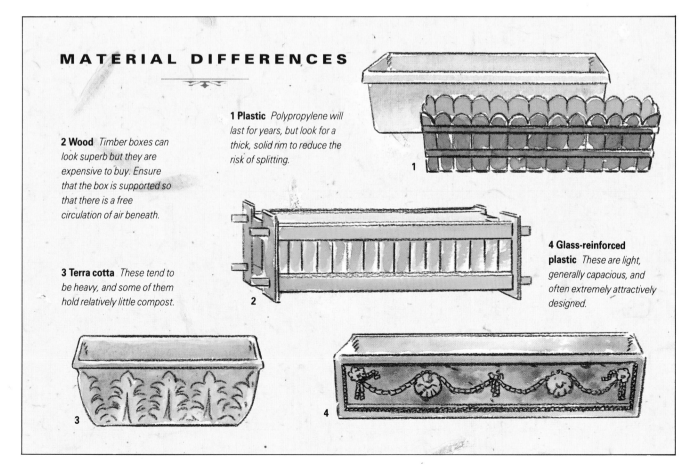

MATERIAL DIFFERENCES

1 Plastic *Polypropylene will last for years, but look for a thick, solid rim to reduce the risk of splitting.*

2 Wood *Timber boxes can look superb but they are expensive to buy. Ensure that the box is supported so that there is a free circulation of air beneath.*

3 Terra cotta *These tend to be heavy, and some of them hold relatively little compost.*

4 Glass-reinforced plastic *These are light, generally capacious, and often extremely attractively designed.*

Stone and concrete troughs can also be used as window boxes. These troughs usually carry ornate patterns, many of them copies from antique pieces. These containers are most appropriate for historic and period houses, since their look is usually not contemporary. They are fairly expensive, and very heavy to move about, but they are quite stately and handsome.

An unusual window box option is to use oblong wire baskets which at least one supplier calls "hayracks." Before planting, line the baskets with overlapping pieces of moistened sheet moss or sphagnum moss to hold the soil mix. These baskets are not as convenient to use as other window boxes, and they dry out even more quickly.

Window boxes are available in garden centers, and in shops located in botanic gardens and other public gardens. Many mail-order nurseries and garden supply companies also sell window boxes, so be sure to check their catalogues.

INSTALLING WINDOW BOXES

Care should be taken when installing window boxes. When filled with plants and soil and then watered, even lightweight plastic boxes are going to be heavy. They must be firmly secured. If your window sill is wide enough, a window box can simply rest upon it. You should anchor the box, though, to make sure it does not slide or blow off the sill. Some cities and towns have regulations governing how window boxes should be mounted, so check this before you begin. If your window sill slopes forward, as many do, you may want to place wedges under the front of the box to level it. To anchor the box securely, attach screw eyes to the window box, and corresponding hooks and eyes on the window frame, or attach the eyes to each other with heavy-gauge wire.

If the window sill is wide enough to accommodate the box without it overhanging then all you need do is fix the box to the window frame or the wall with screws. If the window sill slopes forward, place wooden wedges under the front of the box to make it level.

If the box projects beyond the edge of the window sill, attach brackets to the bottom of the box at the front, and screw the other ends into the wall. If necessary, bend the brackets to fit them around the sill. Make sure you use long enough screws and wall plugs.

If you have narrow window sills, the boxes will most likely overhang the edges. However, you can still put boxes on them, provided you support them underneath with strong metal brackets of suitable size that are fixed to the wall and to the base of the window box. Generally a bracket at each end of a box is sufficient. If your boxes are in a prominent spot you may want to choose decorative brackets, perhaps in fancy wrought iron. Or you could go with something plain and paint them to match the boxes.

Window boxes must have holes in their bases to allow excess water to drain away. In some cases the resultant drips could be a problem unless shallow plastic drip trays are placed under the boxes when they are installed and you are careful not to overwater.

Where window sills are narrow, it is better to mount window boxes on the wall directly below the window. You can place the brackets either on the bottom of the box or on the back. If you live above the ground floor and your window boxes will be viewed from below, you may want to use ornamental brackets of wrought iron or brass.

RINGING THE CHANGES

Inexpensive plastic window boxes, or improvized liners, can be dropped into more impressive outer boxes, or hidden by a false front on the sill. A supply of liner boxes can be planted to follow on and replace earlier ones as they pass their best. Proprietary boxes are available designed to take pots that can be bought ready-planted. With spare pots planted up and waiting in the wings, it is possible to keep a window box looking good almost throughout the year.

❧ **TOP** *Today the trend is for simple designs using few colors. This combination of cream, pink, blue, and gray plants is very tasteful and suitable for the style of the house.*

❧ **LEFT** *Terra-cotta window boxes are popular and an appropriate choice for older-style properties, although they should also be considered for modern homes.*

SUPPORTS FOR CLIMBING PLANTS

Tall plants growing in window boxes, especially in very windy locations, should be supported with dowels or slender stakes. The dowels or stakes can simply be pushed into the soil next to each plant. To avoid damaging the stems, tie the plants loosely to the stakes with soft yarn in a figure-eight pattern.

Climbing plants need support, too, and you can use trellises, strings or wires, plastic netting, or pieces of wood lattice. Trellises are generally made of wood, and you will find them in an assortment of configurations, including grids and fan shapes. A trellis is not going to fit inside a window box, of course, but you can mount it on the wall next to the window if that is where you want to train the vines to grow. Wood lattice and plastic netting can be used the same way. If you do attach a trellis to the wall, put blocks of wood between the trellis and the wall to allow plenty of air to circulate and to provide space for stems and tendrils to twine around the support. Ivy and Virginia creeper will stick to the trellis (or the wall, where its aerial roots can eventually damage bricks or stone) by themselves, but most other vines will need to be fastened to the trellis or guided around strings or wires, at least at first.

A less conspicuous way to support climbers is to train them on strings or wires attached to the back of the window box and to the wall. If you want to train the plants around the window frame, install wires around the frame and fasten the vines to them at intervals.

TOOLS

Window box gardening requires little in the way of tools. All you will need are a few small hand tools: a cultivator to aerate the soil and scratch in granular fertilizers, a watering can, a hand sprayer for misting and foliar feeding, pruning shears or a pruning knife for trimming trees and shrubs and clipping off dead flowers, a small trowel and a dibble for planting seeds.

Securing a window box safely is important at any time, but especially so if used above ground-level. Old houses sometimes have large, flat sills which make them relatively safe, but it is still worth taking additional precautions if there is any chance they could fall and cause injury.

&. A simple but effective way to provide additional security is to fix eye hooks into the windowframe and thread a 1mm galvanized wire through these and small holes drilled through each end of the box. With plastic or metal windowframes it may not be possible to screw in eye hooks, but it should be possible to drill and plug the wall to take them.

&. Sills usually slope slightly so that they shed water more easily. If the slope is steep, cut small wedges from scrap wood to level the box. It is in any case desirable to raise the box off the sill so that air can circulate: there is a risk of the sill rotting if water is allowed to stagnate beneath the box.

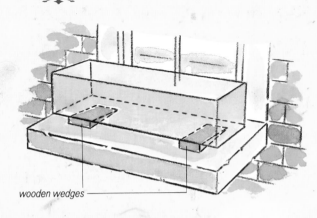

wooden wedges

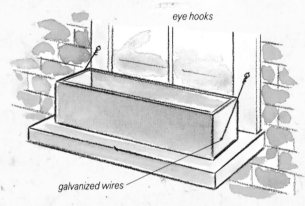

eye hooks

galvanized wires

Brackets It may not be possible to use the sill as in many modern homes it is too narrow, and with casement windows a box would cause an obstruction. However, boxes can sometimes be fitted *below* the window, on special brackets. This is unlikely to be an option for heavy terra-cotta or large glass-reinforced plastic window boxes, but brackets can be bought suitable for many plastic types. Ordinary shelf brackets are unsuitable as they lack the lip on window box brackets that prevents the box slipping or being knocked off. The brackets with lips are screwed to the wall in the normal way. Some brackets can even be used to hang a box on a low wall (far left).

&. When fixing a bracket below a window, allow for the height of the plants when calculating the clearance needed for opening the window.

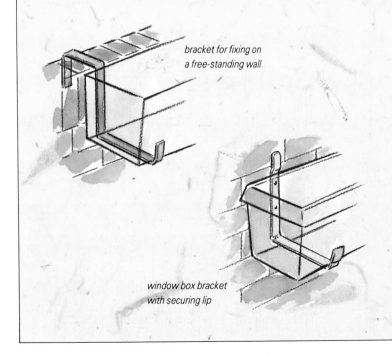

bracket for fixing on a free-standing wall

window box bracket with securing lip

LEFT *Permanent yet seasonal. Permanent dwarf shrubs,* Hebe *and* Hedera *(ivies) can be livened up with a few flowering plants like* Campanula carpatica.

USING TROUGHS

The distinction between window boxes and troughs is not always clear-cut. Many troughs can be used as window boxes if the sill is broad and deep and provided there is absolutely no risk of the additional weight of some of the heavy ones, such as those made from glass-reinforced cement, being unstable or dangerous. Window boxes are generally more modest in size, especially depth and width, but in a suitable setting most window boxes can also be set on the ground as small troughs. Plastic and lightweight materials such as glass-reinforced plastic are particularly suitable where excessive weight is a problem, for instance where sills are narrow or the window box is mounted on brackets.

FINISHING TOUCHES

Plastic boxes are often plain and unattractive. A false front can give them more character. It is also a good way to disguise the use of two small boxes instead of one long one.

A simple front can be made from ¼in (6mm) marine grade plywood cut to the height of the boxes and the width of the window. This can be fixed to the frame, with hooks or to the front of the actual boxes. Seal the ends of the wood, and varnish or paint it to make it look more attractive, perhaps matching the color to that of the paintwork or trim of the house or with an attractive design. For a more rustic finish, fix pieces of bark to the front of the boxes. Or use a front of cross-cut Western red cedar.

CHEAP AND CHEERFUL

Consider using some short-term low-cost "boxes" if you are using a false front, or you can place the containers on a balcony where they will not be very obvious from below. The kind of trays sold for moistening ready-pasted wallpaper are very cheap and hold just as much compost as many window boxes.

Some plastic trays are reasonably robust to handle and will last for a couple of seasons. Those made of expanded polystyrene are much more fragile and should not be moved when full of compost; they are unlikely to be usable for long periods. Make a few holes for drainage in both types.

HOW TO PLANT UP WINDOW BOXES

Lifting a heavy window box into position filled with compost and plants is potentially hazardous. It makes sense to plant up with the box in position whenever possible. Fresh compost should be used for new summer seasonal displays, but for autumn-planted bulbs the old compost can be used as these do not require a high level of nutrients.

The planting plans on pages 74–79 provide plenty of stimulating ideas, but they will have to be modified to suit the size of window box. The distance from front to back, in particular, may cause problems; if there is not enough space to plant the suggested number of rows, either use a box with more generous dimensions or modify the planting plan.

PREPARING TO PLANT

To avoid the risk of waterlogging, always ensure that there are drainage holes in the container, and cover these with broken crocks (pieces of old flowerpots), or broken polystyrene tiles. In deep containers a layer of gravel is placed over the crocks to ensure good drainage and to prevent the compost washing out, but in a shallow window box it is better to use a layer of peat or pulverized bark, which will help to retain moisture while still allowing any excess to drain.

❧ **ABOVE** *The Balkon or Cascade* Pelargoniums *(geraniums) so popular in countries such as Germany, France, and Switzerland, are a distinct type and not the usual ivy-leaved pelargoniums.*

PLANTING A WINDOW BOX

1 *Water all the plants thoroughly an hour or so before planting.*

2 *Arrange the plants on the surface before planting if possible, to make sure the spacing is right.*

3 *Fill to within about 1in (2.5cm) of the top of the window box with a good potting or container compost, and make sure all the rootballs are completely covered (if the tops are exposed they will dry out more quickly).*

4 *Water thoroughly after planting, and for a decorative effect cover the surface with expanded clay granules (these are sometimes sold for greenhouse benches), fine gravel, or pulverized bark.*

Fill the box with compost to within about 1in (2.5cm) of the top.

A light peat-based (or peat alternative) compost is best for window boxes in potentially precarious positions, on brackets beneath the window for example, as it will put less strain on supports. A container compost that includes some loam, or a loam-based compost, is a better choice for window boxes that are absolutely secure and weight is not important (on a broad stone sill on a ground floor window, for example).

PLUNGING POTS

For short-term display, especially in the autumn or early winter, or to provide pockets of fresh interest in a window box that has passed its best, plunge potted plants into vacant spaces for instant results. Ensure the pots are completely covered, and if necessary spread peat or pulverized bark over the top to hide the rims. In the summer, many house and greenhouse potted plants can be used, but harden them off (acclimatize them) to conditions outside in stages.

PLANTING

There are three options for putting plants in window boxes. You can plant directly in the boxes, in removable liners that fit inside the boxes, or in individual pots sunk into peat moss in the boxes. No matter which method you use, be sure every box and liner has drainage holes in the bottom (if your boxes do not have drainage holes you will have to drill them yourself). It is also a good idea to raise the box off the window sill on wood blocks, so

ABOVE Window boxes do not have to be placed on window sills: with suitable brackets they can be used to bring life and color to an otherwise dull wall. To work well, however, it is best to use lots of window boxes so that they form a bold design feature (isolated boxes can look a little sparse on a large wall). Staggering them generally helps to break up an expanse of wall much more efficiently than arranging them in rows.

that air can circulate beneath the box. In stone troughs or other containers in which you cannot make drainage holes, put a layer of gravel in the bottom of the box to improve drainage.

Planting directly in the window box is the simplest approach, but having damp soil in constant contact with the box may damage the window box, especially if it is made of wood or metal. Direct planting also makes it more difficult to remove unhealthy plants (because all the roots intertwine), and to rotate plants in and out of boxes from season to season. However, direct-planting is fine for window boxes that are intended primarily for use in a single season.

Plastic liners offer great versatility. You can plant them and then simply slip them into window boxes; you do not have to take down your boxes to plant them, or lean over the window sill to plant from inside the house.

You can also remove the liners when plants need maintenance, and do your weeding, deadheading, and pruning more comfortably. Spare liners make it easy to start seasonal plantings at the required time and have them ready to replace the previous season's plantings. For example, you can plant summer annuals in liners while your window boxes are full of spring flowers. When summer rolls around your annuals will be nice and full. Switching the liners takes only a few minutes, and your window boxes will always look their best.

Planting in pots also allows you to change individual plants quickly, to show off favorite specimens, or to replace ailing plants. If you move some of your houseplants into outdoor window boxes for the summer, you can slip their pots right into the boxes. It is good idea to surround the pots with peat moss or sphagnum moss to help conserve moisture and to hide the tops of the pots. When you water the potted plants, dampen the moss around them, too. (The moss should be constantly moist, but not soggy.)

Although you have planted your boxes in advance, set the plants on top of the soil before planting to make sure you like the design. Plant window boxes from back to front, putting in the tallest plants first and the shortest ones (or trailers) last. If you are planting one or two small shrubs or trees to serve as focal points, plant them first and then fill in with the smaller plants. If you are planting some bulbs in a box along with several other plants, plant the bulbs last. If you plant them first you could injure them when you dig holes for the other plants. If you are planting vines, put up the trellises or stakes first, then plant the climbers next to them.

When planting your window boxes, be sure to leave enough space between plants to allow them to grow to their full size. If you crowd plants too close together none of them will grow well. If you are transplanting, dig holes large enough to accommodate all the roots. Set the transplants at the same depth they were growing in their previous pot or

🌿 **BELOW** *Wire baskets can be lined but make slits for drainage.*

🌿 **BELOW** *Cheap plastic window boxes can be used to change the display.*

flat. Finally, leave the soil level about an inch below the top of each box, to allow room for watering.

Be mindful of the environmental needs of plants in window boxes, just as you would for plants in garden beds and borders. Because there is less soil to insulate them, plants in window boxes are more susceptible to extreme temperatures than plants growing in the ground. Do not set out tender plants too early, before temperatures have warmed up enough, or they may be damaged.

🍂 **LEFT** *One advantage of making a window box (see page 62) is that it can be painted to suit any taste and colour scheme. By making it large enough to take cheap plastic liner boxes or containers, the plants can be changed round to keep the window box looking bright and beautiful at all times.*

PLANTING PRINCIPLES

Bear in mind the following principles when grouping plants:

🍂 In a mixed planting, use some upright plants to provide height. They do not all have to be in a row at the back – perhaps three evenly spaced toward the rear, or a single one in the center, will be enough to provide punctuation points without looking regimented.

🍂 Bushy or spreading plants should form the backbone of the arrangement, but avoid too many different kinds of plants, otherwise the effect will look fussy and confused. Use mixed colors of one or two types of plants and let the upright and trailing plants provide the contrast in shape and form.

🍂 Generally trailers planted at the front to tumble over the edge and soften the outline add much to a window box, but sometimes it is best to omit them. If the box itself is decorative, make a feature of it by avoiding plants that will obscure its beauty.

🍂 **RIGHT** Erigeron mucronatus *(E karvinskianus). The delicate trails are superb for window boxes, raised urns, and even hanging baskets, where they bring a light texture to stocky plants like dahlias,* Tagetes *and pelargoniums.*

🍂 With the exception of single-subject boxes, which can be extremely effective, as the cascading *Pelargonium* boxes so popular in Switzerland, France and Germany prove, choose a relatively small number of plants but ensure that they contrast in shape, form, and color.

🍂 If seasonal plants are being used, the fewer the types chosen, the more important it is that they have a long flowering period, such as *Impatiens* (busy Lizzie), *Pelargonium*, and *Fuschia*. This is less important in a mixed planting where foliage plants or a succession of blooms from different plants, will hold interest.

🍂 Don't overlook foliage plants – green or variegated.

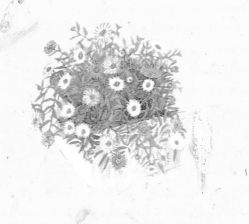

MAKING YOUR OWN WINDOW BOX

Anyone handy with carpenters' tools can easily make wooden window boxes. The advantages here are that not only can you prevent rapid drying out (some ready-made ones are inclined to be on the shallow side), but you can also construct them to fit your window sills exactly.

The best woods for outdoor use are redwood, teak, and western red cedar. These are expensive; cheaper is fir, which will last many years if regularly treated with preservative. Any wood used should be ¾–1in (1.9–2.5cm) thick.

To prevent rapid drying out of the soil make boxes 10–12in (25–30cm) deep. To create well-proportioned boxes make them as wide as they are deep.

If your window sills are very long, do not make one long window box to fit the space because it will be heavy and difficult to handle. Rather, opt for several smaller ones to fit the length of the sill. For instance, if the window is 6ft (1.8m) long, make two 3ft (90cm) long boxes.

There is no need to make elaborate carpenters' joints when building window boxes – simple butt joints will do. Use brass screws of adequate length. If you want extra strength, screw some metal angle brackets on the inside at the corners of the box and where the base joins the sides.

Do not forget to make drainage holes in the base, about 1in (2.5cm) in diameter and 4–6in (10–15cm) apart. Fix two strips of wood, about 2 by 1in (2.5 by 2.5cm), on the underside, one at each end, to slightly raise the box off the window sill and therefore ensure unimpeded drainage of surplus water.

Finally, treat the inside with two coats of horticultural wood preservative. Then treat the outside with preservative, or paint it.

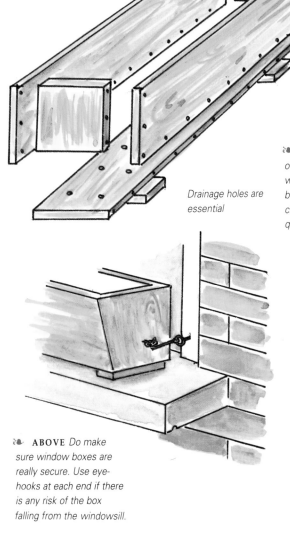

Drill holes for screws

Drainage holes are essential

🐦 **BELOW** *A collection of liners or plastic troughs which fit inside window boxes allows you to change displays easily and quickly.*

🐦 **ABOVE** *Do make sure window boxes are really secure. Use eye-hooks at each end if there is any risk of the box falling from the windowsill.*

ARRANGING PLANTS EFFECTIVELY

Although most window boxes are more or less rectangular in shape, window box gardens should not look flat and two-dimensional. Just like a well-planned garden, these gardens-in-miniature are more interesting when they have depth and variation of plant heights.

Some people make the mistake of planting a single subject and setting the plants in a row. Try to avoid this: it will look too regimented and unimaginative. Aim for more shape in the design by using a mixture of plants of varying sizes and habits.

How much a window box is covered by plants should be determined by the box itself. If it is highly attractive, then it will be a pleasing feature in its own right and should not be covered by plant growth. However, a plain box is best covered with trailing plants.

A row of plants all the same height looks boring and unnatural. In nature plants are not all the same height. Using plants of varying heights will give your window boxes a more naturalistic look. For the best results, plant taller plants in the back of the box, shorter plants in the middle, and low edging or trailing plants in the front of the box to balance the tall plants in the back. Allow trailers to spill over the front of the box to give the box an air of exuberance and charm. Edging or cascading plants and flowers also give the window box a softer, less contrived look. (Nevertheless, remember not to detract from the beauty of the box itself – as noted in the "Planting Principles" on page 61.) Climbing vines planted at the back of a window box can add extra height to a window garden. Support them on a small trellis to one side of the box, or train them to grow up and around the window to frame the view from indoors.

ABOVE In this informal window box, unpruned boxwood (Buxus sempervirens) adds height, white pansies (Viola x Wittrockiana) add mass, and ivy (Hedera helix) trails over the front of the planter to soften its harsh edge.

BELOW Impatiens blooms lavishly in shady spots, and provides masses of color in places too dim for many other plants to flower.

When planting the boxes, do not line up your three sizes of plants in straight rows like little soldiers. For a more flowing, natural look, stagger the plants in the rows, placing some a bit farther back and others slightly forward.

You can also use plant heights to create movement in the window box design. To bring movement to a planting, vary the plant heights from side to side across the box as well as from front to back. You can create a strong, angular direction or a soft curve, depending on how you position the plants.

There are various ways of arranging plants in window boxes. You could go for the pyramidal design: the tallest plants are set in the middle, with shorter and shorter plants grading down to each end. The ends and the front could be planted with trailers if desired.

However, if you feel that tall plants in the middle reduce light inside the house, then place the tallest plants at each end of the box and have lower-growing plants in the middle. Set trailers in front of the low growers.

Finally, take into account the size and shape of the window where the box will be positioned, and keep the plants in scale with the window. Small windows look best with small plants; tall, narrow windows can accommodate taller plants, although the plants should not be so tall that they completely block the windows. If the window is very narrow, consider planting one or two tall plants at one end of the box, and grading to shorter plants at the opposite end of the box. Vines and climbing plants are also particularly attractive when trained around tall, narrow windows.

You can place window boxes on both sunny and shady window sills, but remember that there are temporary and permanent plants that like both kinds of light conditions. If the area is prone to wind, it is best to avoid trailing plants, for these will be lashed around and damaged. Go for sturdy, bushy subjects.

Many people do not take backgrounds into account when creating planting designs. Windows can make rather cluttered backgrounds: there is the framework, probably curtains, and maybe ornaments and pot plants on the window sills indoors. In this situation go for simple designs outside. For instance, choose single-color designs that show up better than mixed colors.

If the background is plain and uncluttered then by all means use mixed colors if you wish. You may wish to keep in mind, though, that single-color designs, coordinated with the house, are quite popular today, especially in contemporary settings. A riot of colors is more appropriate for the traditional English cottage style of garden.

Do not be pressured into thinking that very complicated designs are necessary for window boxes. It is easy to get carried away by the wide range of colorful bedding plants available at garden centers. But often the use of too many different plants creates a fussy, uneasy appearance. Instead, consider comparatively simple designs, using perhaps two or three different kinds of plants.

INDOOR/OUTDOOR WINDOW BOXES

Many houseplants enjoy spending summer outdoors, and a window box makes a good summer home for small and medium-size plants.

A window box planted entirely with houseplants or tropical species can go outdoors for the summer and come back inside in early autumn, before the weather turns cold. If you want to put some houseplants in a window box along with annuals or other outdoor plants, it is easiest to leave the houseplants in their pots and set them into the window box.

COLOR SCHEMES

To achieve the best visual effect with window boxes, it is important to give some thought to the colors you will use in them. Many kinds of color schemes are possible, from soft combinations of pastels to contrasting bold, bright hues. Combining colors in window boxes is much the same as combining them in garden beds. However, because you will be working with a limited number of plants in a small space, the most successful color schemes for window boxes are generally simple ones. There are several basic approaches you can take when mixing colors in your window boxes.

MONOCHROMATIC SCHEMES

Monochromatic schemes – the simplest kind – combine flowers of a single color, or shades of a single color, with the green of foliage and stems. For example, you might opt for an all-yellow garden, or all red, or white. You can add white to a basic monochromatic garden to brighten and add sparkle to the overall look. Window boxes in monochromatic schemes, with or without the addition of white, tend to be calm and serene, and lend themselves to formal planting styles.

▨ **BELOW** *A softer combination in the same color family mixes* Lobelia *from deep purple to palest lavender with* Impatiens *in rose-pink and light pink, and* Fuchsia *in soft pink and white.*

🦋 **ABOVE** *Pinks and purples create wonderful color harmonies in the garden. This window box blends pink and deep purple petunias* (Petunia x hybrida) *with* Lobelia Erinus *in a lighter purple.*

ANALOGOUS SCHEMES

Analogous or related color schemes blend colors that are close to one another on an artist's color wheel, and therefore, harmonize beautifully. Pink and purple is one analogous combination; red, orange, and yellow is another. Pastels usually work beautifully in analogous color schemes. White flowers or silver foliage can be added to lighten and brighten the effect.

CONTRASTING SCHEMES

Complementary or contrasting color schemes are a riskier but interesting approach to mixing hues. Complementary colors are opposite one another on the color wheel. Red and green are complementary, as are blue and orange, and purple and yellow. When a color is placed next to its complement, the effect is to make both colors appear stronger. Such extreme contrasts can easily become jarring in a garden, especially in a small window box. But when sensitively handled, contrasting color schemes can be lively and fun.

The key to success is to choose carefully among the shades and tints of the two colors to find combinations that do not fight each other. You can also use colors that are contrasting without being exactly complementary.

POLYCHROMATIC SCHEMES

Polychromatic or mixed color schemes follow no rules – the choice of colors is strictly up to the whim of the gardener. The cheerful riot of colors found in traditional cottage gardens exemplifies the polychromatic approach.

While mixed color schemes can be lots of fun, they can also easily become chaotic, especially within the confines of a window box. Whatever color scheme you use, consider how the colors will work with the color and the architectural style of your home. Think about the texture of the wall as well as the color of the window frames and doors. If the wall is a dark color, or receives shade for much of the day, use pastels or white-flowered plants in your window boxes. If your wall is white or cream-colored, use bright pastels or rich, strong colors. If your window box will receive lots of sun, bright, strong colors will work best.

SUNNY, SHADY, AND WINDY SITES

Planning an effective window box involves many of the same design considerations as planning a garden bed or border, although in far simpler form. To get maximum visual impact you need to consider the site, environment, and type of plants you desire, just as you do when you plan a garden bed.

An understanding of a few basic principles of garden design will enable you to create sumptuously beautiful window boxes that are perfectly suited to their environment. As with patio containers, spring and summer bedding plants, spring bulbs and other temporary specimens can make very colorful window boxes. Also as with other containers, a few permanent plants can be arranged in window boxes with bedding plants or bulbs planted around them. This gives variation, particularly in shape and texture. One can use dwarf conifers and small evergreen shrubs.

The choice of bedding plants and bulbs for window boxes is the same as for patio containers, with a few additions and deletions. Obviously one would not use very tall plants like Indian shot and castor oil plants in window boxes.

With window boxes it is important to consider designs for both sunny and shady positions, for some parts of the house will be bathed in sunshine all day long and other parts will receive little or none. Sun-loving plants will grow poorly and produce few flowers in shady positions. However, all of these recommended here for shade will also grow in sunny locations.

If you do not want to go to all the trouble of regularly changing planting designs, choose permanent designs instead. Alternatively, you may find some permanent arrangements that you planted in liners useful for filling in gaps between flowering periods. For instance, bear in mind that there may be a gap between spring and summer or autumn winter bedding.

PLANTING DESIGNS FOR SUN

There are plenty of summer designs for sunny positions. The pelargoniums really flower their heads off in sun, and for window boxes there are no finer kinds than the Swiss balcony "geraniums" that provide cascades of blooms all summer. These are the ones that provide much of the summer color on balconies in Switzerland and Austria. They are actually varieties of ivy-leaf pelargonium (*P. peltatum*). The Swiss kinds are so vigorous and floriferous that no other plants are needed with them.

Ordinary varieties of ivy-leaf pelargonium can also be used in window boxes, but as trailers in the front. They look good with bushy heliotrope (*Heliotropium arborescens, H. peruvianum*), which can be used to give height, and with the lower-growing blue ageratum.

Trailing petunias are marvelous plants for window boxes; allow them to cascade over the front. They go well with the bushy zonal pelargoniums. Try orange pelargoniums with blue or purple petunias for a bold effect.

RIGHT *Swiss
balcony geraniums
(varieties of ivy-leaf
pelargonium) provide
cascades of blooms all
summer and need no
other plants with them.
Window boxes that are
high up are generally best
planted with trailers.*

Excellent for providing a summer display
are marguerites (varieties of *Argyranthemum
frutescens* or *Chrysanthemum frutescens*). The
species is a bushy, tender perennial that
produces masses of white daisy flowers
throughout summer. There is also a range of
new cultivars in various colors. Marguerites
could form the main planting, but for
cascading over the edge of the box try
Helichrysum petiolatum, with its gray foliage.

African marigolds (*Tagetus erecta*) also revel
in the sun and make good companions for
marguerites. Tallish marigolds could be used
to create height. Single-color designs are
possible with these two plants.

Permanent planting Minitaure roses, which are
becoming incredibly popular today, are very
nice for summer-long color in window boxes.
Try planting small silver- or gray-foliage plants
with them, such as the cotton lavender
(*Santolina chamaecyparisus* "Nana") or the
lavenders *Lavandula angustifolia* "Munstead"
or *L. lanata*.

Superb designs can be created with dwarf
conifers and heathers. To give height try a
group of *Juniperus communis* "Compressa," a
neat, conical juniper with grayish foliage, and
surround this with heathers for summer,
autumn or winter color.

Other suitable plants for sun include any of
the small, shrubby veronicas or hebes, which
unfortunately are not the hardiest of plants
and may not survive winters in cold climates
unless taken under glass. Most flower
profusely in summer. Dwarf kinds include *H.
albicans*, with white flowers; *H. macrantha*, also
white; and *H. pinguifolia* "Pagei", with gray
foliage and white flowers. Try planting
miniature spring bulbs between them, such as
crocuses, grape hyacinth (muscari), glory of
the snow (chionodoxs) and squills (scilla).
Autumn crocuses would extend the flowering
season still further.

Small culinary herbs are excellent for
window boxes, if you can give them a position
in full sun. A sunny kitchen window sill
would be ideal for the cook.

PLANTING DESIGNS FOR SHADE

For spring, first plant a few small shrubs (which can be left in place until they become too large) like variegated *Eunymus fortunei* and the spotted laurel (*Aucuba japonica* "Variegata"). These could form the middle of the design or could be planted at each end of a box. Then add spring-flowering polyanthus or the more modern colored forms of primrose.

Or try spring-flowering bulbs like small daffodils, grape hyacinths, and scillas growing through a carpet of small-leaved ivy (*Hedera helix* cultivars), which would also cascade over the sides. The ivy can be left permanently in place if desired.

A beautiful summer design for shade features impatiens, or busy Lizzie, the type specially bred for bedding. Contrasting with this could be some spider plants (*Chlorophytum comosum* "Variegatum") with green and white striped grassy foliage. These could be planted near the edges so that they arch over the sides. Spider plants can be kept from year to year, but winter them indoors. To create height in the design, plant some tallish silver-leaved cineraria. You could create a green and white design by using white impatiens – always bearing in mind that they might need even more watering than their neighbors in the window box.

Another popular summer design for shade features pendulous tuberous begonias *Begonia x tuberhybrida* (Pendula group) in various colors. These have to be potted and started into growth in a greenhouse early in the year. They should be planted near the edge of the window box so that they cascade over the side. Use some young plants of the yellow-variegated abutilon (*A. striatum* "Thompsonii") to give height. (The abutilon can be kept in a frost-free greenhouse over winter but will eventually grow too tall for the window box.) By using yellow begonias you will have a pleasing yellow scheme.

Trailing fuchsias are excellent for shady summer window boxes. Plant them near the edges and create height with a bush fuchsia or

two. Spider plants make a superb contrast in shape and color. Alternatively try fresh green asparagus ferns (*Asparagus densiflorus* "Sprengeri") with fuchsias – they will arch over the edge of the box. Keep these from year to year, but winter them indoors.

Many people do not think of using the trailing bellflower (*Campanula isophylla*) outdoors, but it certainly will survive the summer, producing cascades of blue and white flowers. Plant it near the front edge of the box for maximum effect. A trailing foliage plant that contrasts effectively with this bellflower is the white-variegated ground ivy (*Glechoma hederacea* "Variegata"), a hardy perennial. For height in this design use a small plant of New Zealand cabbage palm.

Permanent planting There are numerous small shrubs suitable for shade. An excellent idea is to plant a collection of small shrubs in the boxes for interest at various seasons and to interplant them with small, shade-loving, spring-flowering bulbs like dwarf and miniature daffodil species and cultivars (of which there is a very wide range available) and snowdrops (galanthus). It is best to buy and plant snowdrops immediately after flowering while they are still in leaf, as dry bulbs planted in autumn take several years to settle down and flower well.

🐾 **BELOW** *A pleasing arrangement of plants, which is attractive even before the plants start flowering. A tall fuchsia at one end provides height and lower-growing zonal pelargoniums and fuchsias in the rest of the box have been chosen to avoid cutting out light to the room. Trailing plants, including ivy-leaved pelargoniums, complete the design.*

A particularly popular design consists of *Skimmia reevesiana,* a small evergreen shrub whose white spring blooms are followed by red berries that last all winter, with an edging of the trailing *Lysimachia nummularia* "Aurea," with its yellow foliage, and the lesser periwinkle (*Vinca minor*), which has starry blue flowers in spring. A sprinkling of small spring bulbs can be recommended, too. Unfortunately the skimmia is not a very hardy shrub and is best suited to milder areas (10°F/−12°C and above).

Not many people consider dwarf evergreen hybrid azaleas (rhododendron) for window boxes, but they are ideal for areas in partial shade. They have a low spreading habit and in spring smother themselves with flowers in shades of red or pink, plus white. Lime-free soil that is kept constantly moist is needed. Plant some dwarf lilies between them for summer color.

WINDY SITES

Wind is another important consideration. If your boxes will be located on the side of the house or building that faces into the prevailing winds, concentrate on growing compact, sturdy plants. In very windy locations, you may need to provide stakes or other supports for all your plants. Urban apartment dwellers should think carefully about wind. Tall buildings in cities create strong winds that change speed and direction quickly and often, winds that can tear delicate flowers and leaves right off their stems, leaving plants looking ragged and battered.

If you live in a large city you should pay attention to the quality of the air to which your plants are exposed. Many plants, particularly delicate ones, do not grow well in polluted air.

STRUCTURE TO LAST THE SEASONS

Most window boxes are primarily summertime gardens, but you can also plan them to provide color in spring or autumn, or

even winter in mild climates. The key to success is to plan in advance and choose plants carefully. If you want your window boxes to bloom in spring, in summer, and in autumn, you can grow seasonal plants in individual pots or in plastic liners that you slip into the window boxes when the plants are ready to come into bloom.

One of the most enjoyable parts of planning a window garden is choosing the colors of the flowers and greens you want to have in your box. Many different color schemes are possible in window boxes, and because window gardens are small, it is easy to experiment with different colors from season to season and year to year.

Like conventional gardens, window boxes can be planned to provide interest over successive seasons, or to put on a big display at a particular time of year. You can plan window box gardens to reach their peak in spring, summer, autumn, or all three. If you live in an area where winters are mild, your window boxes can be full of plants in winter as well.

Planning for successions of flowers in window boxes is actually easier than planning a garden bed or border, because window boxes are too small to hold all the plants at once. To plant seasonal window boxes, you will have to plant each season's flowers in separate boxes, pots, or liners, and replace one season's plants with the next. While this means you will have to find places other than your windowsills for plants out of season, you will have the advantage of being able to plan each season's display without regard to the plants that were in your window boxes the season before, or what will follow next season.

SPRING

Where winters are cold, spring is the most welcome time of year, especially for gardeners. Few moments are as rewarding to gardeners as the sight of the first green shoots pushing their way through the surface of the cold earth, whether that earth is in a garden bed or a window box.

OPPOSITE *Pansies start blooming in spring and flower best in cool weather. They are joined here by masses of white Lobelia.*

The first flowers to bloom in spring belong to hardy bulbs, and many of these bulbs grow quite happily in window boxes. The possibilities include *Crocus*, daffodils and narcissus (*Narcissus* species), rich blue *Scilla siberica* and glory-of-the-snow (*Chionodoxa* species), fragrant hyacinths (*Hyacinthus orientalis*), and the shorter-stemmed tulips (*Tulipa* species), especially the Greigii and Kaufmanniana or water lily hybrids. When the plants become crowded after a few years, lift, divide and replant the bulbs to give them more space.

Bulbs are not the only spring flowers that will bloom in window boxes. There are many spring-flowering perennials such as white-flowered candytuft (*Iberis sempervirens*); rock cress (*Arabis* species), which blooms in white or pink; false rock cress (*Aubrieta* species), with flowers of pink or purple; the aptly named basket-of-gold (*Aurinia saxatilis*); horned violets (*Viola cornuta*), in golden orange, cream or purple; and polyanthus primroses (*Primula x polyantha*) in their many shades of red, rose, pink, purple, blue, yellow, and white.

Hardy annuals and biennials also begin to bloom in spring, before the heat of summer sets in. Pansies (*Viola x Wittrockiana*), which come in many shades of yellow, gold, orange, purple, blue, and white, either with or without distinctive face-like markings, bloom beautifully in window boxes. You can buy plants at a local garden center if you prefer not to bother starting seeds yourself. Other good choices are bachelor's button or cornflower (*Centaurea Cyanus*), calendula or pot marigold (*Calendula officinalis*), love-in-a-mist (*Nigella damascena*), Virginia stocks (*Malcomia maritima*), and climbing sweet peas, which also bring the bonus of their heavenly fragrance. Gardeners who live in warm climates can successfully grow these cool-weather annuals for winter flowers.

SUMMER

Summer is prime time for annuals, and besides the ubiquitous geraniums (*Pelargonium* species), petunias (*Petunia x hybrida*), impatiens (*Impatiens* species), and French marigolds (*Tagetes patula*), there are many other summer-blooming annuals to choose from, as well as biennials and perennials that will bloom in the first year.

Blue and purple flowers include flossflower (*Ageratum Houstonianum*); *Browallia speciosa*; cup flower (*Nierembergia hippomanica*); dwarf varieties of *Phlox drummondii*; the very popular *Lobelia erinus*, which can also be had in red or white; globe candytuft (*Iberis umbellata*); and mealycup sage (*Salvia farinacea*). A pretty plant for a shady box is the wishbone flower, *Torenia Fournieri*.

Red, rose and pink summer flowers include snapdragons (*Antirrhinum majus*), pyrethrum or painted daisy (*Chrysanthemum coccineum*), *Verbena* species, *Cosmos*, China asters (*Callistephus chinensis*), wax begonia (*Begonia x smeperfloren-scultorum*), zinnias (*Zinnia elegans*), *Fuschia*, flowering tobacco (*Nicotiana* species), creeping Madagascar periwinkle (*Catharanthus roseus*), field poppies (*Papaver Rhoeas*), and globe amaranth (*Gomphrena globosa*). In hot, dry locations, try growing the daisylike flowers of ice plant (*Mesembryanthemum crystallinum*) or the brilliantly colored and low-growing moss rose (*Portulaca grandiflora*).

If you want yellow and orange flowers, consider nasturtiums (*Tropaeolum majus* or *T. minus*), the climbing canary creeper (*Tropaeolum peregrinum*), *Coreopsis*, *Celosia*, African daisy (*Arctotis stoechadifolia*), cape marigold (*Dimorphotheca* species), and calendulas.

White summer flowers include honey-scented sweet alyssum (*Lobularia maritima*), which also comes in pink, lilac, and purple; Shasta daisies (*Chrysanthemum maximum*); and white varieties of *Petunia*, *Begonia*, *Pelargonium*, and *Impatiens*.

Some summer bulbs that are suitable for window boxes are tuberous begonia (*Begonia x*

tuberhydrida*), whose showy double flowers light up a shady spot with warm, rich reds, yellows, oranges and pinks; and dwarf cultivars of *Dahlia*, which bloom from late summer well into autumn, depending upon the variety.

AUTUMN

The classic autum flower is, of course, the hardy chrysanthemum (*Chrysanthemum x morifolium*), whose warm-toned flowers echo the colors of autumn foliage. In addition, you can choose mums with purple, white, or pink flowers. The best chrysanthemums for window boxes are compact varieties such as cushion, pompon, or button mums. Because the plants are quite demanding and do not grow well for everyone, you may find it easiest to buy new plants for your window boxes each autumn rather than trying to winter them over.

If chrysanthemums do not hold great appeal for you but you still want autumn flowers, try planting autumn bulbs – autumn crocus and colchicum (whose flowers resemble large crocuses). These bulbs are planted in summer to bloom in a matter of weeks.

🍂 **ABOVE**
Chrysanthemums are autumn classics in gardens and window boxes.

SUMMER BOXES
AND TROUGHS

For some people the window box or veranda trough is their only opportunity to garden outdoors. For others, boxes and troughs are used on a large scale for massed effect. Whatever the situation this type of container provides the scope to use a very wide and exciting range of plants.

Most of the designs shown here follow a simple formula using a generous helping of trailing plants to hang over the edge. Upright plants are used toward the back and the more spreading subjects fill in between. "Architectural" or "dot" plants are sometimes incorporated to add emphasis. These basic principles aside, the designs can be simple or complex as desired.

❧ BELOW Three good "doers" used in a simple design of mixed colours. Ingredients for a 36in (90cm) trough:
1 Impatiens *(busy Lizzie) x 9*
2 *mixed* Pelargonium *x 9*
3 *mixed trailing lobelia x 12*

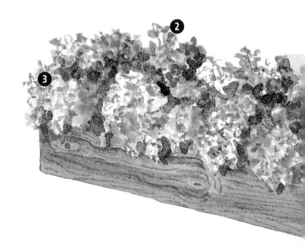

❧ BELOW Reds and pinks, with whites and a blue, this is a collection of reliable varieties. Ingredients for a 30in (75cm) trough:
1 *mixed* Begonia semperflorens *(fibrous-rooted begonia) x 8*
2 Pelargonium *"Apple Blossom rosebud" x 2*
3 Lobelia erinus *"Red Cascade" x 6*
4 Brachycome iberidifolia *x 2*
5 *ivy-leaved* Pelargonium *"Sugar Baby" x 2*
6 *white* Petunia *x 2*

❧ RIGHT Brighten up even the dullest spots with the riotous yellow of Tagetes *and trailing* Bidens. *This red brick wall provides an ideal contrast to the flowers.*

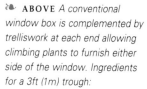

🌿 **ABOVE** *A conventional window box is complemented by trelliswork at each end allowing climbing plants to furnish either side of the window. Ingredients for a 3ft (1m) trough:*

1 *plum-colored* Petunia *x 6*
2 *bush* Fuchsia *x 2*
3 *lilac-blue trailing* Lobelia *x 10*
4 *white-flowered ivy-leaved* Pelargonium *x 2*
5 Plectranthus *x 3*

6 *trailing* Fuchsia *x 2*
7 Brachycome iberidifolia *x 4*
8 *blue annual morning glory* (Ipomoea) *x 4*
9 Impatiens salmon *"Impulse Blush" (busy Lizzie) x 6*

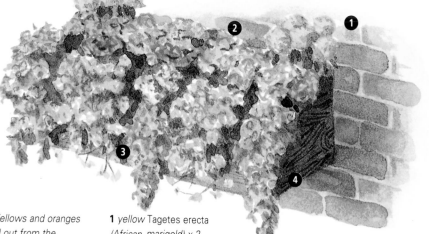

🌿 **ABOVE** *Yellows and oranges certainly stand out from the crowd, blue tones down the overall effect. Ingredients for a 30in (75cm) trough:*

1 *yellow* Tagetes erecta *(African marigold) x 2*
2 *mixed* Tagetes patula *(French marigold) x 15*
3 Bidens ferulifolia *x 2*
4 Convolvulus mauritanicus *x 3*

🌿 **ABOVE** Fuchsia, Tropaeolum *(nasturtium)* and Pelargonium *(geranium)*. Effective displays can be created by carefully combining plants with striking leaves. Although most will produce flowers these are normally regarded as a bonus but beware, they might spoil the color scheme or steal the show.

🌿 **RIGHT** *The plants used are more tolerant to dry compost than most – but they still need regular watering to do well. Ingredients for a 3ft (1m) trough:*
1 Antirrhinum *"Floral Carpet"* (snapdragon) x 10
2 *mixed* Pelargonium x 5
3 *white* Agyranthemum frutescens *(marguerite)* x 2
4 Convolvulus mauritanicus x 1
5 Sedum lineare *"variegatum"* x 3
6 *pink-flowered ivy-leaved* Pelargonium x 3
7 Bidens ferulifolia x 1
8 *mixed* Portulaca grandiflora x 5

🌿 **RIGHT** *The arrangement gives the display increased height and depth to create a more striking effect than that on one level. The trailing ivies in this design could be left* in situ *and the flowering plants changed seasonally. Ingredients for a 36in (90cm) pair of troughs:*
1 Salvia splendens x 6
2 *mixed* Impatiens *(busy Lizzie)* x 12
3 *mixed* Petunia x 4
4 Hedera helix *"Glacier"* (silver-variegated ivy) x 5
5 *white* Begonia x tuberhybrida x 6

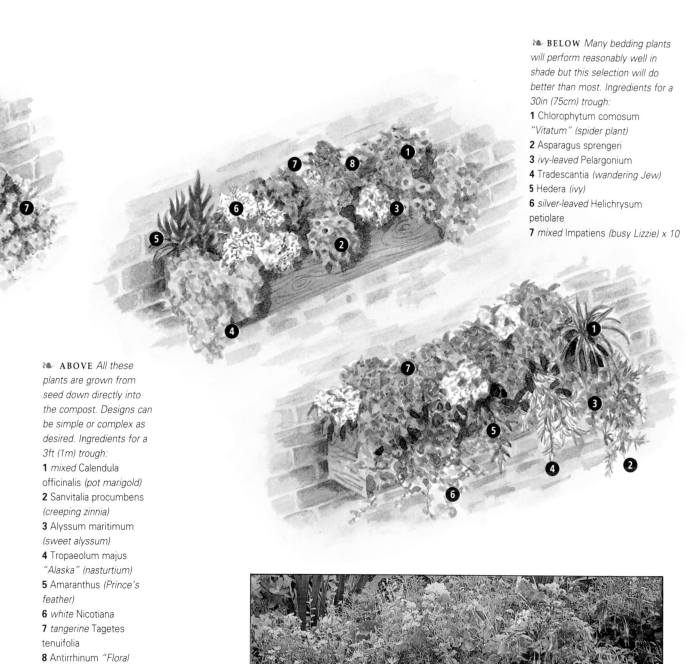

7

🐚 **BELOW** *Many bedding plants will perform reasonably well in shade but this selection will do better than most. Ingredients for a 30in (75cm) trough:*
1 Chlorophytum comosum *"Vitatum" (spider plant)*
2 Asparagus sprengeri
3 *ivy-leaved* Pelargonium
4 Tradescantia *(wandering Jew)*
5 Hedera *(ivy)*
6 *silver-leaved* Helichrysum petiolare
7 *mixed* Impatiens *(busy Lizzie) x 10*

🐚 **ABOVE** *All these plants are grown from seed down directly into the compost. Designs can be simple or complex as desired. Ingredients for a 3ft (1m) trough:*
1 *mixed* Calendula officinalis *(pot marigold)*
2 Sanvitalia procumbens *(creeping zinnia)*
3 Alyssum maritimum *(sweet alyssum)*
4 Tropaeolum majus *"Alaska" (nasturtium)*
5 Amaranthus *(Prince's feather)*
6 *white* Nicotiana
7 *tangerine* Tagetes tenuifolia
8 Antirrhinum *"Floral Carpet" (snapdragon)*

🐚 **RIGHT** *Trailing* Fuchsia, Lobelia, *and* Bidens *lead the way in this cascade of floral delight. The trough from which they grow has long been obscured.*

ROMANTIC AND FORMAL SCHEMES

There is no specific criterion that defines what is meant by a romantic window box, but many window boxes do create a decidedly romantic impression. Romance is a quality – a general feeling – imparted by the plants, the containers, and the setting. The overall impression is one of lushness, delicacy, and sensuality. Romantic window boxes appeal to the senses rather than the intellect. They delight the eye with a profusion of greenery of varying shapes and sizes, and flowers in soft pastel shades or a mix of bright, lively colors. Fragrant flowers are ideal for romantic boxes. You can also plant foliage and blossoms of varying textures to appeal to the sense of touch. Formal window boxes, by contrast, stress order and discipline to achieve a cool sophistication.

ROMANTIC SCHEMES

Romantic window boxes are not about straight lines and sharp angles. Instead, these plantings are full of soft curves and natural, irregular shapes. Diagonal stems and branches add movement and life to the design. The most romantic-looking window boxes are lush with plants allowed to tumble together in playful disorder, like a somewhat overgrown garden. Trailers and ground covers such as periwinkle (*Vinca minor*) and English ivy (*Hedera helix* cultivars) spill over the edges of the container. Flowering vines entwine as

BELOW *The tiniest imaginable planter holds just two* Lobelia Erinus *plants, one sweet alyssum* (Lobularia maritima), *and a single wax begonia* (Begonia x semperflorens-cultorum), *whose colors gleam like jewels in a niche in a plain brick wall.*

RIGHT *This large box or raised bed features a wide variety of foliage and flowering plants blended together. Ingredients for a 7ft (2.1m) x 36in (90cm) container:*

1 Canna x generalis
2 *white* Nicotiana *x 3*
3 Lobelia cardinalis *x 3*
4 Salvia farinacea *"Victoria" x 6*
5 *bush* Fuchsia
6 *pink* Osteospermum *x 5*
7 *mixed* Begonia x tuberhybrida *x 7*
8 *blue trailing* Verbena *x 3*
9 Heliotropium arborescens *(cherry pie) x 3*
10 Convolvulus mauritanicus
11 *pink* Diascia *x 6*
12 *white* Argyranthemum frutescens *(marguerite) x 3*
13 Felicia amelloides *x 3*
14 *mixed* Impatiens *(busy Lizzie) x 8*
15 *Amaranthus (*Prince's feather*) x 3*
16 *blue* Plumbago capensis
17 Tanacetum ptarmiciflorum *x 5.*

SUMMER BOXES AND TROUGHS

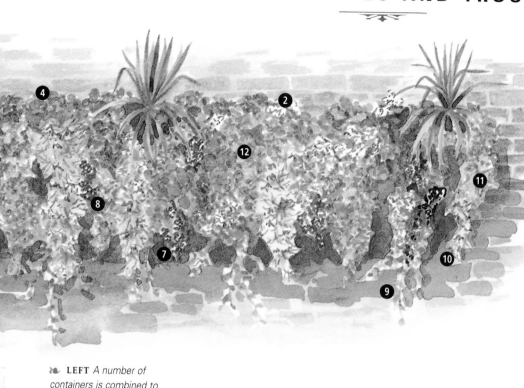

LEFT *This 13ft (4.2m) long set of troughs makes a real impact.*
Ingredients:
1 Cordyline *x 3*
2 *mixed* Impatiens *(busy Lizzie) x 20*
3 *mixed* Pelargonium *x 16*
4 *mixed* Petunia *x 16*
5 *trailing* Fuchsia *x 4* ·
6 *mixed pendulous* Begonia x tuberhybrida *x 4*
7 *blue trailing* Lobelia *x 25*
8 Brachycome iberidifolia *x 8*
9 Plectranthus *x 4*
10 Lotus berthelotii *x 4*
11 *deep pink* Verbena *x 4*
12 Calceolaria *"Sunshine" x 12*

LEFT *A number of containers is combined to create a bank of color supplied by Alyssum, Petunia, and Hedera (ivy). The display is in scale with the buildings, whereas a single run of troughs would have been too insignificant to make an impact.*

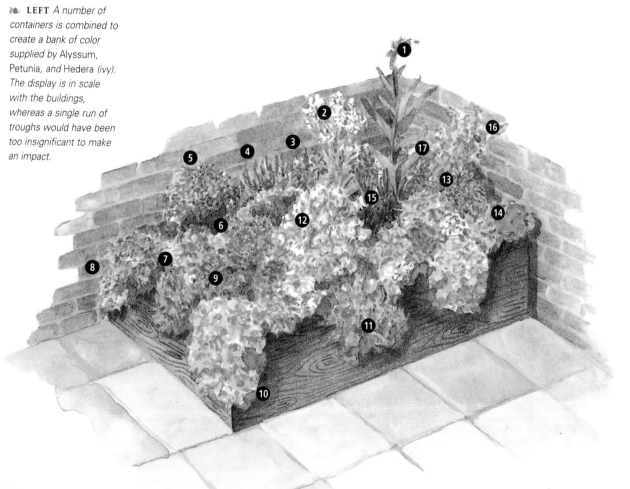

they climb the wall or window frame above the box. Inside the container, delicate foliage and old-fashioned flowers intermingle their colors and scents in cheerful abandon.

Plant forms in a romantic window box tend to be delicate. A romantic garden does not look sleek or contemporary, but instead conveys a sense of gentleness and nostalgia. This is not the place for bold, sculptural plants like yuccas or bromeliads, which make dramatic statements. It is also not the place for meticulously pruned shrubs and conifers, or for topiary or plants trained as standards. To achieve a romantic look, allow the plants to assume, as much as space will permit, their natural shapes and growing habits. Basic maintenance like picking off spent flowers is important, but leave precise pruning for formal gardens.

One particularly evocative way to create a feeling of romance is to echo aspects of traditional English cottage gardens. Obviously you cannot have a true cottage garden in a window box. But you can adapt some of the features – old-fashioned flowers, mixed color schemes – to create a look reminiscent of a cottage garden.

Old-fashioned flowers to consider for window boxes include spicy-scented garden pinks (*Dianthus* species), sweet William (*Dianthus barbatus*), Johnny jump-up (*Viola tricolor*), pansies (*Viola x Wittrockiana*), violets (*Viola odorata*), fuchsia (*Fuchsia* cultivars), candytuft (*Iberis* species), bachelor's button or cornflower (*Centaurea Cyanus*), flowering tobacco (*Nicotiana alata*), nasturtium (*Tropaeolum minus* or *T. majus*, the climbing type), feverfew (*Chrysanthemum Parthenium*), calendula (*Calendula officinalis*), the fragrant wallflower (*Cheiranthus Cheiri*), English primrose (*Primula vulgaris*), French marigold (*Tagetes patula*), Iceland poppy (*Papaver nudicaule*), and Shirley poppy (*Papaver Rhoeas*). Roses are another traditional cottage garden plant, and if they appeal to you, you can grow one of the miniature varieties.

Flowering vines to try for a romantic effect include morning glory (*Ipomoea purpurea*), the closely related night-blooming moonflower (*Calonyction* species), fragrant wisteria (*Wisteria sinensis*), exotic passionflowers (*Passiflora* species), sweet-scented honeysuckles (*Lonicera* species) and jasmines (*Jasminum* species), black-eyed Susan vine (*Thunbergia alata*), canary creeper (*Tropaeolum peregrinum*), and sweet peas (*Lathyrus odorata*), with their intense, spicy-sweet fragrance.

FORMAL SCHEMES

Formal gardens stress order and symmetry, with straight lines and sharp angles creating a sense of stability and stillness. The same qualities found in formal gardens can be achieved on a miniature scale in window boxes. Formal window boxes are best suited to period homes and buildings, particularly in urban areas.

To achieve the necessary feeling of repose, a formal window box needs balance and stability. To create an elegant effect, design the window box on a strong horizontal axis punctuated with equally strong verticals. Avoid diagonals that would create a feeling of movement, and flowing curves that would encourage the viewer's eye to move from one part of the planting to another when observing the box.

You might start with a small evergreen in the center rear of the window box, or perhaps a row of three small trees in a larger box to provide a vertical focal point. The trees should be pruned into neat, perfect shapes. If you want a formal look without using trees or shrubs, you can design a symmetrical planting of flowers and foliage plants. Some variation of plant heights is important to add interest to the design, but try to keep the design simple and orderly. Concentrate on placing taller plants in the back of the box and shorter plants in front.

Formal window boxes require scrupulous maintenance to have them look their best at all times. If plants become overgrown, the elegant lines and forms disappear, and the planting looks unkempt.

Containers for formal window gardens can be either sleekly elegant (fiberglass, for example, or wood painted white or dark neutral color) or an antique style (such as a stone or concrete trough with a classical motif).

Dwarf evergreens are the plants most often used for vertical accents in formal window boxes. Good candidates include dwarf cultivars of boxwood (*Buxus sempervirens*), false cypress (*Chamaecyparis* species), juniper (*Juniperus* species), bay laurel (*Laurus nobilis*) in mild climates, and for large boxes, hollies (*Ilex* species). Some gardeners like to grow plants trained as standards – neat balls of foliage atop straight, bare stems. Rosemary (*Rosmarinus* species) is one possibility although it must be moved indoors over winter in cold climates. Geraniums (pelargoniums) and chrysanthemums (*Chrysanthemums x morifolium*) can also be trained as standards.

Many kinds of flowers can work in formal window boxes, but the best choices are plants with neat growing habits. Upright plants such as geraniums (pelargoniums), tulips (*Tulipa* species and hybrids), and daffodils and narcissus (*Narcissus* species and hybrids) work well, as do plants that form compact mounds, like impatiens (*Impatiens* species).

🌿 **ABOVE** *The trailing ivy is kept carefully in bounds here, and it is balanced by a* Lobelia *on either side.*

CHAPTER THREE

HANGING GARDENS

The Hanging Gardens of Babylon were one of the Seven Wonders of the Ancient World, and we can only wonder about the marvelous effect they had. Still, with a bit of ingenuity you can inject a note of wonder around your own property with colorful displays overflowing from hanging baskets or wall pots. Some knowledge about the shape and timing of different flowers can help you produce vivid "balls of color" suspended in the air.

LEFT *Large daffodils
are not usually throught of
as being suitable for
hanging baskets, although
as can be seen here they
do make a very effective
display. It is important to
avoid letting the soil
freeze solid over
prolonged periods in the
winter.*

CHOOSING AND USING HANGING BASKETS

Traditionally hanging baskets are made from a widely spaced mesh of strong galvanized wire and are bowl-shaped. They are generally supported with three chains. Plants can be planted right through the wires in the sides to create a ball of color. Such wire baskets are inclined to dry out rapidly in warm weather, so frequent watering is a must – at least twice a day.

Modern hanging baskets are generally made from molded plastic and are again bowl shaped and supported with chains. Some include a built-in drip tray and others have a water reservoir to cut down on the frequency of watering. Being nonporous they do not dry out as rapidly as wire baskets.

One of the drawbacks of molded-plastic baskets is that you cannot insert plants in the sides. So unless you plant some very long trailing plants, quite a lot of the basket is visible. And the bottom of a plastic basket is not one of the most pleasing sights!

No matter what type of basket you choose, select larger rather than smaller ones, because the smaller they are, the quicker they dry out.

Small baskets also very much restrict planting designs. The largest baskets are at least 12in (30cm) in diameter and have a depth of 6–8in (15–20cm.

There are numerous places to hang baskets. House walls are the most obvious places, but they can also be hung in porches and used to decorate garages and sheds. Do not set them too high, or you may have problems with watering. It is also important to avoid windy spots: strong winds can do a lot of damage to baskets and plants.

Choose metal brackets to support hanging baskets and make sure they are securely screwed to the wall or other support. Baskets are quite weighty, especially when they have just been watered.

WALL POTS

These pots look like flower pots or other containers that have been cut in half so that they can be mounted flat against walls. They can be used like hanging baskets, and an advantage over hanging baskets is that they do not sway around in the wind, so they can be used in more exposed areas.

The majority of wall pots are made from terracotta. Being made of clay, they are inclined to dry out rapidly in warm weather. They come in various shapes and sizes and are comparatively inexpensive. (For an idea of the range available, and how they can be displayed, see the illustrations on pages 78–79.)

Rather more expensive are lead wall pots in traditional styles. These are very much "at home" on the walls of period houses.

There are also metal half baskets for mounting flat against walls – reminiscent of hay baskets for horses. These can be lined with black plastic sheeting before being filled with soil. You can make slits in the plastic and plant through the sides.

ABOVE *Wall-mounted baskets make excellent containers for colorful summer bedding such as petunias, lobelia and impatiens, which have been planted through the sides of the container to hide it, as well as in the top.*

LEFT *With traditional wire hanging baskets you can create balls of color with plants such as impatiens, lobelia, and ivy-leaved pelargoniums, as they can be planted all around the container.*

🍂 **ABOVE** *Unlike hanging baskets,
terra-cotta wall pots do not sway around
in the wind but since they do not hold
much soil they can dry out quickly.
However, they have the advantage of
being attractive, even when empty.*

CONTAINERS IN THE AIR

Hanging baskets, hanging pots and wall
baskets and wall pots all make use of space
that would otherwise be wasted. Although
these containers often require much more
attention than window boxes and tubs – being
more exposed and generally holding less
compost, they dry out more quickly – they are
invaluable where space is very limited, and
even in a courtyard garden can bring an
otherwise uninteresting wall to life.

If you do not want to fix a lot of containers
directly on to the wall (which involves a lot of
masonry drilling and plugging), fit a stout
wooden trellis to the wall, and hang wall pots
to this.

MATCHING THE SEASON

Plants chosen for hanging baskets and wall
pots are usually temporary bedding plants
that bloom for one particular season, generally
summer. There are some permanent plants
that can also be used, if desired. Bear in mind
that in areas where the temperature drops
below 25°F/−4.5°C it can be difficult to winter

any plants in baskets or wall pots outdoors
because the soil quickly becomes frozen solid
in freezing weather. If you wish to overwinter
planted baskets and pots, keep them in a cool
but frost-free greenhouse.

FOR SUMMER

Many people plant glorious mixtures of
summer bedding plants in baskets and wall
pots: trailing lobelia, sweet alyssum (*Alyssum
maritimum*) with its masses of white flowers,
and petunias, with perhaps zonal
pelargoniums or bush fuchsias in the center,
maybe with silver-leaved cineraria. There is
nothing wrong with such designs and indeed
they look most attractive in a traditional
cottage-style garden, but the trend is toward
simpler designs using fewer plants, and even
toward single-color designs coordinated with
the house colors.

As with window boxes watch the
background. If it is cluttered, go for plants of
one color. If plain, then by all means use
plants in mixed colors if you wish.

For shady locations use plants in light
colors, such as pale yellows, cream, white,
light pinks, and so forth, as they will show up
much better than strongly colored plants.

Popular basket plants for the shade are
pendulous fuchsias and pendulous tuberous
begonias (*Begonias x tuberhybrida*, Pendula
group) plus the bedding impatiens or busy
Lizzie. You could have a bushy centerpiece of,
say, silver-leafed cineraria, or perhaps a
clump of green and white striped spider plant.

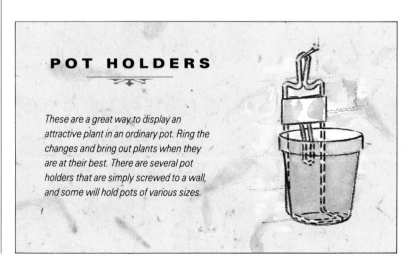

POT HOLDERS

*These are a great way to display an
attractive plant in an ordinary pot. Ring the
changes and bring out plants when they
are at their best. There are several pot
holders that are simply screwed to a wall,
and some will hold pots of various sizes.*

HANGING
GARDENS

RIGHT *Wall pots do
not have to be featured
alone but can be
combined with climbing
plants such as jasmine
and roses. This one
contains a variegated ivy
that does not dominate its
container.*

EXERCISING
THE
IMAGINATION

*The ground rules for how best
to display hanging baskets are
loose, and with a little
imagination you can multiply
their effect brilliantly. Used in
conjunction with other
containers or simply en masse,
hanging baskets can provide
an explosion of color.*

RIGHT *Vibrant
flowers spring from every
conceivable fitting. Ivy-
leaved* Pelargoniums,
Tropaeolum *(nasturtiums),
and* Petunia *dominate the
scene and thrive on this
sunny wall. The display is
at its peak in summer, but
seeds can be sown
directly in the baskets in
mid-spring, once the
threat of frost has gone.*

BASKETS AND POTS

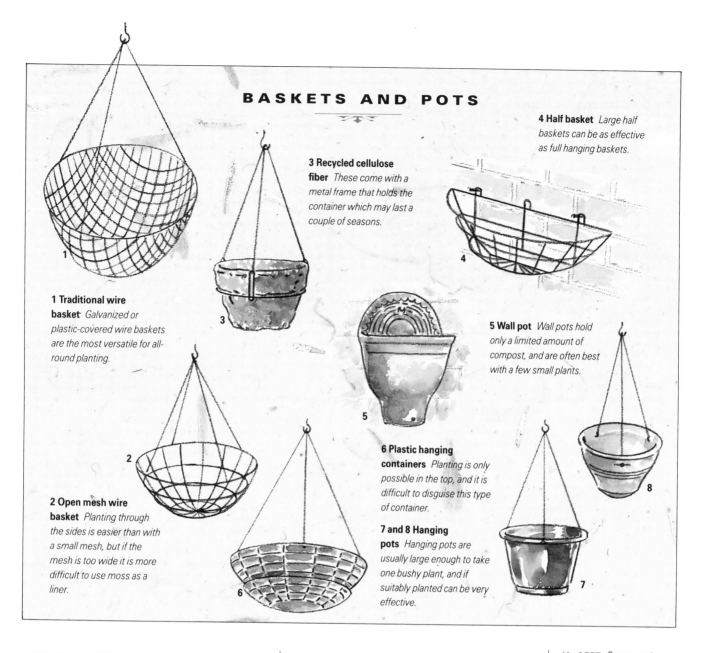

4 Half basket *Large half baskets can be as effective as full hanging baskets.*

3 Recycled cellulose fiber *These come with a metal frame that holds the container which may last a couple of seasons.*

1 Traditional wire basket *Galvanized or plastic-covered wire baskets are the most versatile for all-round planting.*

5 Wall pot *Wall pots hold only a limited amount of compost, and are often best with a few small plants.*

6 Plastic hanging containers *Planting is only possible in the top, and it is difficult to disguise this type of container.*

2 Open mesh wire basket *Planting through the sides is easier than with a small mesh, but if the mesh is too wide it is more difficult to use moss as a liner.*

7 and 8 Hanging pots *Hanging pots are usually large enough to take one bushy plant, and if suitably planted can be very effective.*

ABOVE *An old manger that once held hay for horses now has another use. Often improvized containers are useful because they hold plenty of compost. This display contains lobelia, trailing pelargonium, cascading fuchsia, and tropaeolum (nasturtium).*

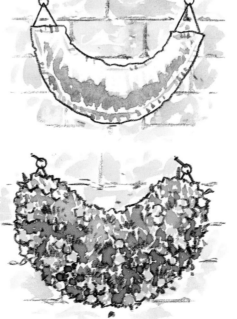

LEFT *Swags make a novel way to grow plants. The bags, made in a range of shapes including garlands, tubes, and drops, come complete with compost. Suitably compact plants, such as Impatiens (busy Lizzie), are planted through small slits made in the covering and grown on a flat surface (such as a greenhouse bench or on the ground) for a month before hanging. They are suitable only for one season and could be home-made.*

LINERS

❧ **ABOVE** *Basket liners (left to right): moss; whalehide liner with capillary mat; polyurethane foam; cellulose fibers.*

Sphagnum moss is the traditional basket liner, and still one of the best – but it is preferably brought while still fresh and alive. Unless you keep it constantly damp it will soon die and turn an unattractive brown. The big advantage of moss is that it is so adaptable and plants can be inserted anywhere in a wire basket with ease.

Polyethylene is often used because it is cheap and readily available (you can even cut up an old plastic bag). Black polyethylene is usually chosen, but only on visual grounds. It is difficult to line a basket neatly with polyethylene and wrinkles are almost inevitable, so slit the sheet and overlap it as necessary. To plant through the sides, simply slit the polyethylene as required. Once well covered with plants, polyethylene is acceptable, but it is very unattractive during the early stages of growth.

Coir fiber liners are made from jute and coconut fiber. They look rather like a

coconut on one side and sacking on the other. The coconut fiber side faces outward. They will last more than a season, but planting through the side is not easy.

Polyurethane foam liners are also available and easy to use, and are made in various sizes. They last for several seasons, and planting between the slits is easy.

Recycled cellulose fiber liners must be used in wire baskets designed to take them, otherwise they will not fit properly. Moss is a better choice for a wire basket, and if you don't want to plant in the sides a normal plastic basket may be a better choice.

Whalehide (bitumized cardboard) liners are made in a range of sizes to fit particular baskets. Plants can be inserted through the sides where the slits occur and some have a capillary matting disk at the base to help retain water.

LEFT *Without
hanging baskets, this
display of pots would
seem rather flat; they
however, in combination
they provide a stunning
21m (7ft) high
extravaganza. An
abundance of blue trailing
lobelia helps to link the
petunias at the lower level
with the ivy leaved
pelargoniums in the
baskets. A common
colour theme throughout
unifies the display.*

Summer-flowering pansies are highly recommended for baskets and will flower well in partial shade. They can be obtained in separate colors, so they are ideal for single-color designs. Or try blue and white pansies with silver-leaved cineraria if you want a "cool" design.

Plants that need sun include multiflora or small-flowered petunias, ivy-leaved pelargoniums, verbena hybrids, and lobelia, all of trailing habit. For bushy growth try the bedding calceolarias (*Calceolaria integrifolia*) with their masses of small yellow flowers. If you want a flower that spreads, there are gazanias, which revel in hot, dry conditions. A particularly pleasing design includes yellow calceolarias as a centerpiece, with yellow, gray-leaved gazanias around the edge.

Zonal pelargoniums make a good center-piece for trailers like petunias and verbenas. Or plant a bushy heliotrope with pink or red ivy-leaved pelargoniums.

For something a bit more unusual try dwarf bushy nasturtiums (*Tropaeolum majus*); these are hardy annuals that have brightly colored flowers in shades of red, orange, yellow, pink, and white. Seeds of these can be sown directly in the baskets in mid-spring. They do best in full sun.

Black-eyed Susan (*Thunbergia alata*) is an excellent half-hardy annual for hanging baskets or wall pots. The rounded yellow flowers have a "dark eye," or center, and are produced freely from early summer to early autumn. They do best in full sun.

FOR SPRING, AUTUMN, AND WINTER

Pansies are now becoming very popular basket plants, especially those that bloom throughout winter in mild areas and well into spring. What is more, they tolerate partial shade. Try a combination of winter pansies and trailing ivies (the latter are permanent plants).

Other useful bedding plants for spring flowering are double-flowered daisies and polyanthus, or colored primroses. Once again provide contrast in shape and color by

planting trailing ivies around the edge of the basket. Both of these plants are shade tolerant.

Permanent trailing plants for spring-flowering are cultivars of periwinkle (*Vinca minor*) with starry blue, purple, or white flowers, suitable for growing in shade or partial shade. Try growing miniature spring bulbs in the center of the basket.

For winter color try cultivars of *Erica carnea* (*E. Herbacea*) in sunny positions. The flowers of this heath come in shades of pink, red, or white. No other plants are needed with them.

Another winter-flowering heath is *Erica x darleyensis*. This comes in similar colors, but an especially attractive cultivar is "Silberschmeize" ("Molten Silver"), with its white flowers carried in very long spikes from late autumn until mid-spring in mild areas.

Conveniently, both of these heaths are lime-tolerant, though they grow better in lime-free soil. The heaths are permanent plants and can be kept in baskets for several years. To keep them compact trim off the old, dead flower heads in the spring before new growth commences.

Autumn is a time when hanging baskets can be colorless, but they need not be if you plant them with dwarf chrysanthemums, especially the suncharms and American cushion mums.

Camellias in baskets An extremely unusual but nevertheless interesting and appealing idea has recently emerged from New Zealand – growing camellias in hanging baskets. At first this sounds impossible because most camellias are eventually large, upright, bushy shrubs. However, small but flowering-size plants of somewhat trailing or pendulous habit can be planted (one per basket) and the young growths trained, by judicious tying, to grow outward and downward, over the edge. Obviously when a plant starts to outgrow a basket it can be taken out and planted in the garden. Camellias in baskets would also make pleasing features in a cool greenhouse or conservatory.

ABOVE A typical summer design for a hanging basket: bushy pelargoniums and French marigolds surrounded by impatiens or busy Lizzie. Other plants for creating height include heliotrope (which is sweet-scented) and dwarf African marigolds (which are not!).

BELOW Campanula isophylla "Bellflower." An outstanding hanging basket or window box plant because of its trailing stems and the cooling effect of its blue flowers in a hot summer.

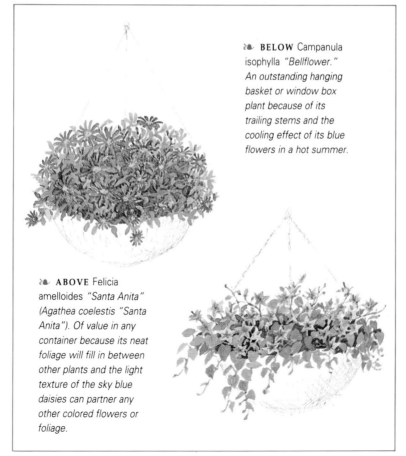

ABOVE Felicia amelloides "Santa Anita" (Agathea coelestis "Santa Anita"). Of value in any container because its neat foliage will fill in between other plants and the light texture of the sky blue daisies can partner any other colored flowers or foliage.

PLANTING UP HANGING BASKETS AND WALL POTS

Hanging baskets are the most difficult containers to grow well. They demand much more care than tubs, troughs, and window boxes, and being in an exposed position require much more thorough acclimatization before being set in position. Getting the right mix of plants is also more difficult than in a window box or tub.

Planting plans later in the book provide dependable ideas for a range of different planting styles, but these must be adapted to the type and size of container being used. Moss-lined wire baskets are the most versatile, enabling side planting to be achieved easily. Recycled cellulose fiber hanging containers can be planted in the sides by cutting out small triangular holes. Solid plastic containers enable plants to be inserted in predetermined positions in the sides, but the vast majority of plastic hanging containers only permit planting in the top.

Trailers are much more important for "baskets" with solid sides, as most are viewed from a low angle. Planting all round the sides of a moss-filled basket can produce a globelike mass of flowers and foliage.

PREPARING TO PLANT

Water all plants, whether in pots or seed trays, a couple of hours before planting. If possible prepare supports in a sheltered position or glasshouse from which the planted basket can be hung – it is inadvisable to put a basket in its summer position straight after planting.

Compost weight is vitally important for hanging baskets. Loam-based composts are generally too heavy. Peat-based composts or their alternatives are more suitable, though they are even more demanding regarding watering and feeding.

PLANTING

The step-by-step illustrations opposite show the principles of planting a wire basket. For a solid basket, follow the general advice from step four.

Good camellias for growing in baskets are the free-flowering cultivars of *C. x williamsii*. These bloom in the spring, producing flowers in shades of pink, red, or white.

Camellias must be grown in lime-free soil, ideally an all-peat type, and they thrive in partial shade. Make sure the plants are in a position that does not receive early morning sun, as this can damage frozen flower beds.

Do bear in mind that in areas subject to cold winters (10°F/−12°C and below) it would be advisable to hang planted baskets in a cool but frost-free greenhouse during frosty or very cold weather, otherwise plants may be damaged or killed, especially if the soil ball remains frozen for a long period.

PLANTING A WIRE BASKET

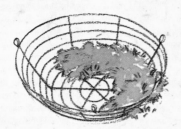

1 Many modern baskets have a flat base, which means they can be stood on a bench for planting.

2 Place sphagnum moss about 1in (2.5cm) thick in the base and up the sides to the first level for side planting.

3 Add compost to this level. Then insert small plants through the sides. Less damage will be done to the plants if the foliage is fed through the mesh from the inside rather than the roots pushed through from the outside.

4 Add more moss to the sides, and bring the compost to the level of the next row of plants.

5 For the top, set the central plant in position first – this is often pot-grown and the rootball should be placed with the minimum of damage before the other plants are set around it. Plant any trailing plants next.

6 Finally infill the top with bushy plants. Use fingers to pack them between the roots of the other plants; it is generally easier than trying to use a trowel. Finish off the top of the basket with a thick layer of moss (or fine stone chippings).

SMALL HOLE, BIG PLANT

Commercially, baskets are often planted with small seedlings in "plugs" (small wedges of compost) that are easily inserted through a small aperture. Plants purchased in late spring or early summer will be much larger and more difficult to plant.

Small-leaved plants can usually be threaded through, but those with larger and perhaps brittle leaves, such as Begonia semperflorens (fibrous-rooted begonias), need a different technique. Roll the leaves up in a small square of polyethylene or paper, rather like rolling a cigarette. The resulting tube will go through quite small holes.

HOOKS AND HANGERS

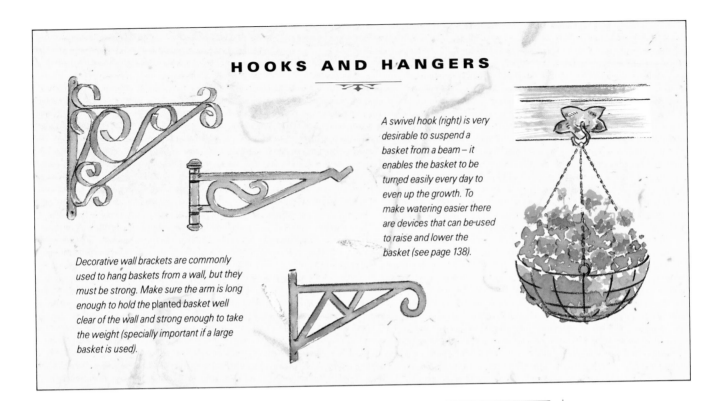

A swivel hook (right) is very desirable to suspend a basket from a beam – it enables the basket to be turned easily every day to even up the growth. To make watering easier there are devices that can be used to raise and lower the basket (see page 138).

Decorative wall brackets are commonly used to hang baskets from a wall, but they must be strong. Make sure the arm is long enough to hold the planted basket well clear of the wall and strong enough to take the weight (specially important if a large basket is used).

❧ **LEFT** An advantage of a wire-mesh hanging basket lined with moss is that it is very easy to plant all round the sides, which helps to produce a ball-like effect even with compact plants such as Begonia semperflorens (fibrous-rooted begonia). This basket is particularly interesting, however, as an example of how a planting with two different species can work well if their growth habits are compatible. Browallia speciosa has been interplanted with the begonias to provide a much fuller and more interesting texture than would be produced by the begonias alone. See opposite for inside tips on building a ball of color.

CREATING A BALL OF COLOR

Generally lightweight soils are best for baskets and wall pots, so all-peat potting soil is recommended.

WIRE BASKETS

When planting a wire basket first line the inside to hold in the soil. Traditionally wire baskets are lined with sphagnum moss, and aesthetically this is still the best. Alternatively you could use a synthetic medium for a liner; there are a number of different ones available. Use according to the manufacturer's instructions. Black plastic sheeting can also be used; punch some holes in the bottom for drainage.

Once the basket is lined it can be planted. To make this job easier for you, steady the basket by standing it on top of a larger flower pot.

The arrangement of plants, especially summer bedding plants, generally has trailing kinds planted in the sides and around the edge, and upright, bushy kinds in the center. To accomplish this, first place a shallow layer of soil in the bottom of the basket, lightly firm it, and then insert some trailing plants through the wires so that their roots rest on the soil surface. If you are using plastic or some other synthetic liner you will have to make slits in it so that you can push the roots through. Sphagnum moss can simply be parted with the fingers to make room for roots. Then add more soil and lightly firm it. Then add more soil and lightly firm it. Insert some more trailers, then position the busy plants in the centre. Fill in with more soil and finally plant trailers around the edge. Make sure you leave a space of 1in (2.5cm) between the soil surface and the top of the basket so that there is room for watering.

Wall baskets are planted the same way.

MOLDED-PLASTIC BASKETS

With molded-plastic baskets simply add soil to about half the depth, lightly firm it, then position some bushy plants in the center, followed by trailers around the edge. Fill in with more soil and lightly firm it. Do the same for wall pots.

After planting, gently water the plants thoroughly to settle them in, using a watering can fitted with a sprinkler.

PLANTING SCHEMES FOR SUMMER BASKETS

There are few more glorious floral spectacles than a well-grown hanging basket. Yet there are few more disappointing sights than its parched remains in mid-August. Such disappointment is avoidable if you follow the "Practical Tips" on page 96.

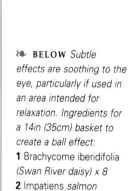

🍂 **ABOVE** *This combination of startling contrasting colors presents an eyecatching, almost dazzling effect. Ingredients for a 14in (35cm) basket:*
1 *10 deep pink* Verbena *x 2*
2 *Yellow pendulous* Begonia x tuberhybrida *x 5, planted in top only*

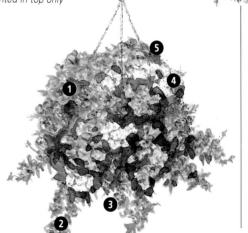

🍂 **BELOW** *Subtle effects are soothing to the eye, particularly if used in an area intended for relaxation. Ingredients for a 14in (35cm) basket to create a ball effect:*
1 Brachycome iberidifolia *(Swan River daisy) x 8*
2 Impatiens *salmon "Blush" (busy Lizzie) x 8, alternately planted.*

LEFT *A small but well-chosen range of colors using several different plants can provide a delicate effect. Ingredients for a 14in (35cm) basket:*
1 *pink* Impatiens *(busy Lizzie) x 5*
2 *red- and white-flowered ivy-leaved* Pelargonium *x 2*
3 *blue trailing* Verbena *x 5*
4 *white* Alyssum *x 10*
5 *blue* Petunia x hybrida *x 5*

As well as the traditional hanging basket, wall baskets, corner baskets and mangers all provide the opportunity to lift color above ground level and add an extra dimension to almost any area.

Many plants make suitable basket subjects, a few are almost indispensable. Trailing varieties are particularly valuable as they greatly contribute to the character and charm of a hanging container.

The following designs offer a range of ideas which can, of course, be adapted to suit individual tastes. The suggested numbers of plants per basket will provide a very full effect. Where possible choose plants that have been grown in small pots, 4in (10cm) or less, so as to allow enough room for their roots as well as plenty of fresh compost. If larger plants are used reduce the numbers but still fill in between with smaller plants such as lobelia.

Before planting a basket remember it will need to be watered regularly until disfigured by frost or cold winds. This effort will be well rewarded with a lovely display lasting for five months or more.

PRACTICAL TIPS

Watering is the key to success and a few basic points should be kept in mind. These tips can be overlooked all too easily by people concerned with instant effects – don't forget that for plants, too, water gives life:

Ensure the lining of the basket is high at the edges and the compost surface slopes down toward the center, as this makes watering much easier.

The more the plants grow, the more water they'll consume. During summer they get very thirsty!

Walls and other buildings shelter baskets from rain. Remember to water these baskets even in wet weather.

Consider installing an irrigation system for your baskets – it will make an amazing difference.

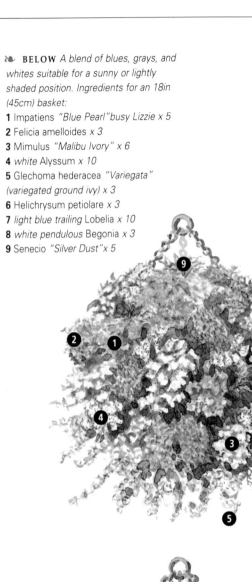

BELOW *A blend of blues, grays, and whites suitable for a sunny or lightly shaded position. Ingredients for an 18in (45cm) basket:*
1 Impatiens *"Blue Pearl"* busy Lizzie x 5
2 Felicia amelloides x 3
3 Mimulus *"Malibu Ivory"* x 6
4 white Alyssum x 10
5 Glechoma hederacea *"Variegata"* (variegated ground ivy) x 3
6 Helichrysum petiolare x 3
7 light blue trailing Lobelia x 10
8 white pendulous Begonia x 3
9 Senecio *"Silver Dust"* x 5

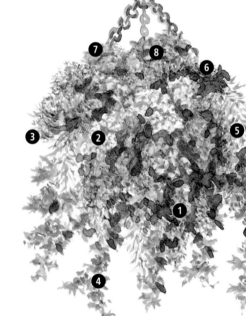

🌿 **BELOW** *Only the top is planted making this display suitable for the solid type of basket. Trailing plants take the eye away from the hard lines of the container.* Ingredients for a 14in (35cm) basket:
1 *purple* Impatiens *(busy Lizzie) x 2*
2 Lobelia *"Sapphire" x 5*
3 *red- and white-flowered ivy-leaved* Pelargonium *x 2*
4 Helichrysum petiolare *"Limelight" x 2*
5 *white* Begonia semperflorens *x 3*
6 Petunia *"Sky Blue" x 3*
7 *lavender* Pelargonium

🌿 **ABOVE** *The white-flowered, ivy-leaved Pelargonium "L'Elegante" and the lilac-blue Brachycome combine wonderfully to produce an air of romance and tranquility.*

🌿 **LEFT** *A delectable range of pinks sprinkled with blues and silver.* Ingredients for an 18in (45cm) basket:
1 Lobelia *"Lilac Cascade" x 10*
2 Impatiens *salmon "Impulse Blush" (busy Lizzie) x 5*
3 Lotus berthelotii *x 5*
4 *rose-colored* Pelargonium *x 3*
5 *pink trailing* Fuchsia *x 3*
6 Brachycome iberidifolia *x 5*
7 *pink* Diascia *x 5*
8 *lilac* Petunia *x 6*

🌿 **BELOW** *Planted in a 14in (35cm) half basket and suitable for a shady spot.*
1 Begonia *"Illumination"x 3*
2 *lavender* Pelargonium *x 3*
3 *blue trailing* Lobelia *x 10*
4 *silver-leaved* Helichrysum petiolare *x 2*

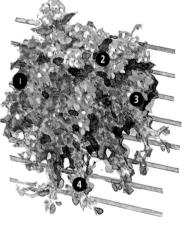

🌿 **BELOW** *The sprawling plants used in this design will allow a container to furnish quite a large area of wall.* Ingredients for a 16in (40cm) wall basket:

1 *pink* Diascia *x 3*
2 *deep pink* Verbena *x 3*
3 *white-flowered ivy-leaved* Pelargonium *x 2*
4 *trailing* Plectranthus *x 2*
5 *trailing white* Lobelia *x 8*
6 *mixed white* Impatiens *(busy Lizzie) x 3*
8 *variegated* Pelargonium

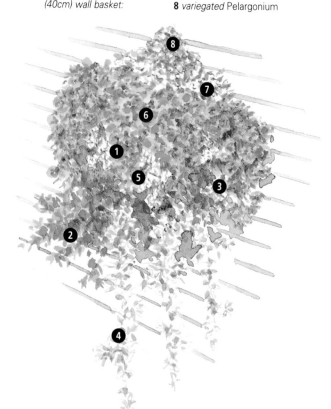

LEFT *Although still requiring water to flourish, the plants included here are more tolerant of sporadic watering than most – but don't get complacent. Ingredients for a 16in (40cm) basket:*

1 *mixed* Pelargonium *x 5*
2 Convolvulus mauritanicus *x 3*
3 Bidens *x 3*
4 Hedera helix *"Glacier" ivy x 2*
5 *white-flowered ivy-leaved* Pelargonium *x 2*
6 Sedum lineare *x 5*

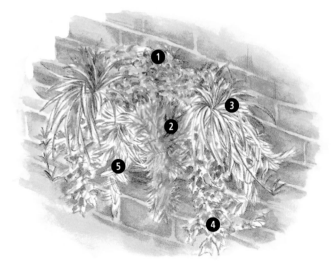

ABOVE *Several houseplants are suitable for outdoor use in summer. Most of these are tolerant of shade and inconsistent watering, although in a fairly light position and given copious water, this design will produce a luxuriant display. Ingredients for a 14in (35cm) wall basket:*

1 Impatiens *mixed (busy Lizzie) x 5*
2 Asparagus sprengeri *x 2*
3 Chlorophytum comosum *(spider plant) x 2*
4 Hedera helix *(ivy) x 2*
5 Tradescantia *(wandering Jew) x 3*

ABOVE *Some very delicate effects can be achieved by using a selection of shades and textures in blue. Ingredients for a 16in (40cm) three-quarter or corner basket:*

1 Brachycome iberidifolia *"Tinkerbell" x 3*
2 *dark blue trailing* Lobelia *x 12*
3 Impatiens *"Blue Pearl" (busy Lizzie) x 5*
4 *variegated* Glechoma *x 2*
5 *mauve-flowered ivy-leaved* Pelargonium *x 2*
6 Verbena *"Blue Knight" x 5*
7 *blue* Petunia *x 6*
8 Felicia amelloides *x 3*

RIGHT *A cheerful selection of mixed colors, but water generously for good results. Ingredients for a 20in (50cm) quarter- or hay basket:*

1 *silver-leaved* Helichrysum petiolare *x 6*
2 *rose-pink-flowered ivy-leaved* Pelargonium *x 10*
3 Mimulus *"Malibu Mixed" x 12*
4 *mixed* Pelargonium *x 5*

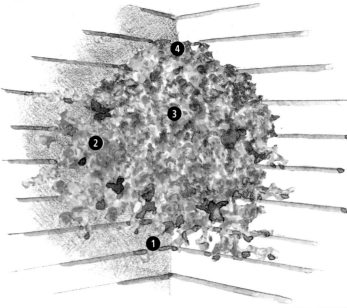

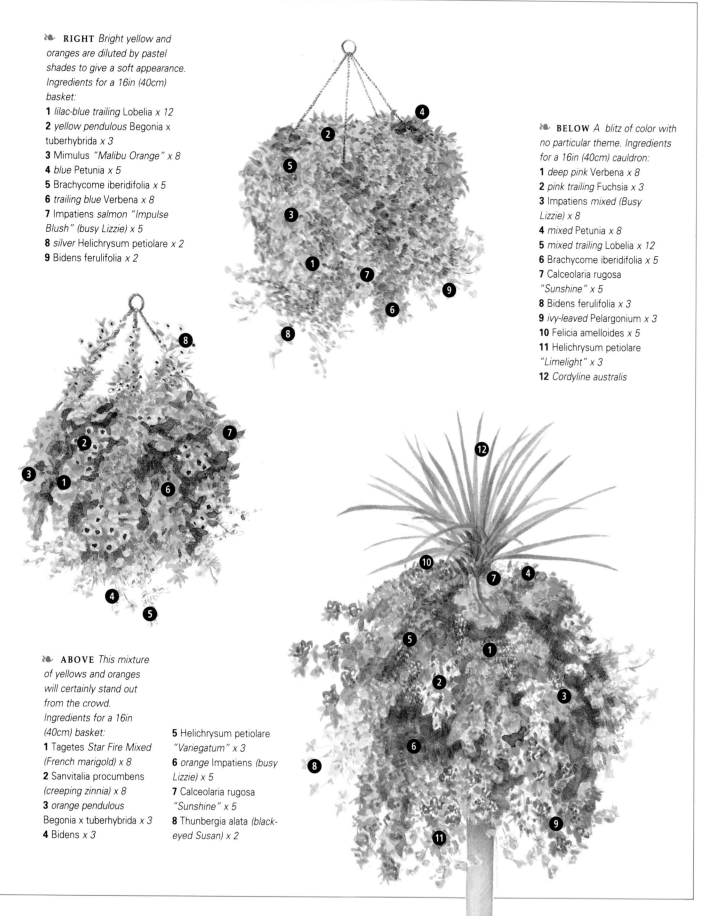

RIGHT *Bright yellow and oranges are diluted by pastel shades to give a soft appearance.* Ingredients for a 16in (40cm) basket:
1 *lilac-blue trailing* Lobelia *x 12*
2 *yellow pendulous* Begonia x tuberhybrida *x 3*
3 Mimulus *"Malibu Orange" x 8*
4 *blue* Petunia *x 5*
5 Brachycome iberidifolia *x 5*
6 *trailing blue* Verbena *x 8*
7 Impatiens *salmon "Impulse Blush" (busy Lizzie) x 5*
8 *silver* Helichrysum petiolare *x 2*
9 Bidens ferulifolia *x 2*

BELOW *A blitz of color with no particular theme.* Ingredients for a 16in (40cm) cauldron:
1 *deep pink* Verbena *x 8*
2 *pink trailing* Fuchsia *x 3*
3 Impatiens *mixed (Busy Lizzie) x 8*
4 *mixed* Petunia *x 8*
5 *mixed trailing* Lobelia *x 12*
6 Brachycome iberidifolia *x 5*
7 Calceolaria rugosa *"Sunshine" x 5*
8 Bidens ferulifolia *x 3*
9 *ivy-leaved* Pelargonium *x 3*
10 Felicia amelloides *x 5*
11 Helichrysum petiolare *"Limelight" x 3*
12 Cordyline australis

ABOVE *This mixture of yellows and oranges will certainly stand out from the crowd.* Ingredients for a 16in (40cm) basket:
1 Tagetes *Star Fire Mixed (French marigold) x 8*
2 Sanvitalia procumbens *(creeping zinnia) x 8*
3 *orange pendulous* Begonia x tuberhybrida *x 3*
4 Bidens *x 3*
5 Helichrysum petiolare *"Variegatum" x 3*
6 *orange* Impatiens *(busy Lizzie) x 5*
7 Calceolaria rugosa *"Sunshine" x 5*
8 Thunbergia alata *(black-eyed Susan) x 2*

CHAPTER FOUR

WORKING
WITH WATER

Creating a mini-pool, complete with water lilies and other aquatic plants, in a large tub or similar container is easily accomplished and makes a pleasing feature on a sunny patio or even on a balcony or flat roof. Water adds new dimensions to a garden: there is movement when wind ruffles the surface of the water, and there are reflections when it is calm. Sun glinting on the water adds to the atmosphere.

SUITABLE CONTAINERS FOR WATER GARDENS

A good size for a small pool is something around 3ft (90cm) in diameter, about the size of a wooden tub or half-barrel. You may find other containers of suitable size, such as large circular concrete tubs. The pool should be at least 18in (45cm) deep, so avoid any very shallow containers.

Obviously these containers need to be waterproof, but this is easily accomplished by lining them with a butyl-rubber pool liner. Alternatively use one of the cheaper plastic pool liners. Incidentally black is a good color for a liner – it creates a sense of depth in a pool.

The simplest arrangement is to stand the water container right on pavement, pebbles, or bare soil. If you are quite ambitious, you could cluster a group of mini-pools – perhaps three – together. This arrangement would create more impact than a single pool and, of course, give you more scope for growing plants.

You could also sink mini-pools to their rims in soil alongside a patio with their edges disguised by flat pieces of rock. This not only creates a more natural appearance but ensures the water temperature does not fluctuate wildly, as happens when tubs are above ground.

Suitable moisture-loving plants can then be planted in the surrounding soil which is generally kept moist by the pool overflowing periodically when it rains or when you replenish it with fresh water. Typical plants for the pool surrounds include astilbes, with plumes of feathery red, pink or white flowers in the summer; plantain lilies (hostas) with their bold foliage; and bog primulas, with candelabras of yellow, orange, pink, or red flowers in summer.

It is best to choose small plants, or miniature versions of plants, for the surrounds so that they are in scale with the pool and do not swamp it visually.

Plastic containers are the easiest to use. Most readily available are various kinds of shrub

tubs or large indoor plastic plant containers (those intended for indoor use are best as they are less likely to have drainage holes in the base). Some plastic containers have thin sections in the base that can be punched out for drainage but are supplied watertight. This kind of container is ready for immediate use! Simply fill with water and plant.

The size and appearance of a plastic container are important. The surface area should be as large as possible, so bucket-shaped containers are unsuitable. A rectangular container will not only look better, it will probably have a larger surface area to depth ratio (a broad, shallow container is infinitely better than a tall, narrow one).

ABOVE *A wooden tub or half barrel is easily turned into a mini-pool, complete with water lilies and other aquatic plants, creating an unusual feature for a sunny patio, balcony or roof garden. Do not place it underneath a tree as fallen leaves will rot and pollute the water.*

Unless the pool is to be plunged in the ground, colour should always be considered. Dark brown or even black work well and do not detract from the plants; whites and bright colours seldom look good. Small ready-made pond containers can also be used. These are round, rectangular, or free-form.

Half barrels Wooden half barrels have more charm than plastic containers, but making them waterproof can be tricky. As genuine barrels were obviously waterproof when they were used for their original purpose there is no reason why they can't be so again even if they have been sawn in half. Unfortunately they may have been allowed to dry out for some time which causes the wood to shrink.

Try to make the barrel waterproof again by keeping it moist. Soak it in a pond for a few days; otherwise fill the barrel with a hose and keep topping it up periodically. This may be enough to swell the wood to make the barrel waterproof again.

Usually other remedial action is necessary. A caulking material or a mastic sold for sealing aquariums can be used to fill gaps betwen the staves. Choose a black one, and make sure the barrel is dry first. A combination of this

and the natural swelling of the wet wood is usually sufficient to make even a rather poor barrel waterproof.

A really inferior quality barrel may not respond to this treatment, and for these a liner of black butyl rubber is the best solution. To avoid the inevitable severe kinks and folds becoming a major problem in such a small container, make a few slits in the liner to get a better fit, and join the overlap with a butyl liner repair kit (these work rather like a tire repair patches). Neatly trim the liner level and staple it to the sides around the rim.

Old glazed sinks can be used as miniature ponds, but they usually look best if fully or partially plunged into the ground, as they are not especially elegant. Above ground, it may be necessary to raise the sink on a couple of bricks to ensure that it is level.

The plug, if still available, can be used to retain the water but it should be glued into position with a suitable waterproof adhesive, such as a PVA glue, and, if necessary, an aquarium sealer too. If there isn't a plug, buy one from a hardware shop. The overflow will need to be blocked if the water level is to be raised to the rim of the sink.

PLUNGED POOLS

Half barrels, stone sinks and troughs are attractive features that should be displayed in a prominent position. Plastic containers and glazed sinks are best plunged fully or partly into the ground as their beauty lies primarily in the plants. Even an old washing up bowl can be given a new lease of life this way, perhaps planted with a miniature waterlily.

MAKING A BARREL POOL

1 Fill the cut-down barrel with water (or soak it in a pond) to allow the wood to swell and make watertight joints.

2 If after a few days it still leaks, empty the water out, leave the barrel to dry, then fill any areas that leak with a waterproof mastic.

3 If the barrel is in very poor condition it may be necessary to line it with butyl rubber. As this is black it will not be too conspicuous once the barrel is planted.

FILLING AND PLANTING THE CONTAINER

The planting period for aquatics is between mid- and late spring. Most people will prefer to plant water lilies and other aquatic flowers. Small baskets are adequate for the plants recommended here.

Heavy loam is the best soil to use for aquatics. Place some in the bottom of the basket, firm it well, then set a plant in the middle and fill in with more loam, again firming well. Finish off with a layer of pebbles to prevent the surface being washed away.

Then gently lower the baskets into the water. It is best not to lower newly planted water lilies to the full depth to start with. At

first lower them so that only a little water covers their crowns. Then lower them gradually as they grow. This is most easily accomplished by standing the baskets on bricks and then removing the bricks one at a time as the lilies get larger. Miniature water lilies can be grown in water as shallow as 12in (30cm).

The other aquatics described in this chapter are marginal plants and only need a few inches (centimeters) of water over their roots. Grow them around the edge of the tub.

The alternative way to grow water lilies and other aquatics is directly in a tub with no basket. Plant them in a 4–6in (10–15cm) deep layer of heavy loam placed in the bottom of the water container. The loam can be mounded up the sides of the tub for the marginal plants.

Now to the arrangement of plants in a tub. One miniature water lily will be adequate for a 3ft (90cm) diameter pool. Place it in the center so that it has space to spread its leaves.

Some submerged oxygenating plants or "water weeds" such as water milfoil (*Myriophyllum* species) should also be planted in the center of the pool because they help to keep the water clear. These usually come in small bunches, and a couple of bunches will be adequate for a tub. Then set the marginal plants around the edge of the tub.

🙋 **RIGHT** *Water lilies and other aquatics can be planted in special plastic lattice aquatic baskets. The crown of each plant should be at soil level.*

🙋 **RIGHT** *There are several miniature water lilies that are suitable for cultivation in a tub, as well as numerous small restrained marginal plants such as variegated sweet flag with its grassy foliage.*

LEFT Water lilies (some of which have fragrant blossoms) not only add color to a mini-pool but help to shade the water, important if fish are to be introduced. All pools should also contain submerged aquatics to oxygenate the water and help to keep it clear.

FAR LEFT Mimulus or monkey flower is a bog plant which will happily grow in shallow water. The summer flowers may be orange, red, or yellow.

LEFT The mini water lily Nymphaea pygmaea "Helvola" is popular for tiny pools, the yellow flowers showing up well against the dark leaves.

MINIATURE WATER LILIES

These are the most popular miniature water lilies.

Nymphaea x Pygmaea cultivars – The smallest of all is "Alba", which has white flowers 1in (2.5cm) in diameter and small, deep green oval leaves. "Helvola" produces small, bright yellow flowers, each with a conspicuous boss of orange stamens. The blooms show up beautifully against the dark olive green, purple, and brown mottled leaves.

Millpond water lily (*Nymphaea odorata minor*) – This small plant has beautifully scented starry flowers in pure white, no more than 3in (8cm) in diameter. These are carried on attractive reddish brown stems. The leaves are medium green above and deep red underneath.

Pygmy water lily (*Nymphaea tetragona*) – This is a very tiny species with white flowers and golden stamens, about 2in (5cm) in diameter. The oval leaves, 3–4in (8–10cm) across, are blotched with brown when young, and the undersides are red.

MARGINAL AQUATICS

One must be extremely careful when choosing marginal aquatics for a tub because some are very vigorous and tall. The following small-growing kinds, of restrained habit, can be recommended with confidence for the mini-pool.

Acorus gramineus "variegatus" – A cultivar of the sweet flag, this plant has grassy foliage which is variegated cream and deep green. The flowers are insiginificant. Unfortunately this is not one of the hardiest marginal aquatics; indeed, it is not completely frost-hardy.

Double marsh marigold (*Caltha palustris* "Flore Pleno") – This is one of the favorite marginals because of its colorful and long-lasting displays. It is a dwarf, compact plant with fully double, bright golden yellow flowers over a long period in spring and early summer. The bright green, shiny foliage makes an excellent background for the blooms.

Bog bean (*Menyanthes trifoliata*) – The bog bean thrives in shallow water and between early spring and early summer produces white flowers with fringed petals. The deep green leaves, composed of three leaflets, make an excellent background for the distinctive "hairy" blooms.

Water forget-me-not (*Myosotis scorpioides*) – This aquatic variety is rather like the familiar bedding forget-me-nots, except that it thrives in shallow water. It differs from bedding forget-me-nots, too, in that it has smooth rather than hairy foliage. The rather loose flower heads consist of pale blue flowers that bloom for most of the summer. This is a popular and very easily grown marginal plant that will help to hide the edge of the pool.

Double-flowered arrowhead (*Sagittaria sagittifolia* "Flore Pleno") – The distinctive foliage of this plant is arrow shaped, hence the popular name. In late summer double white flowers are produced.

🐾 **ABOVE** *The double marsh marigold (Caltha palustris "Flore Pleno") is a favorite marginal plant for small and mini-pools. It flowers in the spring and enjoys full sun, as do all aquatics.*

🐾 **ABOVE** *The bog bean s unusual hairy flowers make a good contrast to other aquatic blossoms.*

CARE OF THE POOL AND PLANTS

The water in a newly created pool will quickly turn green with algae and become like pea soup. To many people this is, of course, devastating. But people familiar with pools will not worry about it, for they know that the water will gradually become clear of its own accord, provided the pool has been well planted with submerged oxygenating plants and other aquatics.

On no account change the water when it becomes green, otherwise the problem will never solve itself. The fresh water will simply become green again. Just leave the pool alone to settle down and remember that once the plants are established the water will gradually clear up. As water evaporates the pool should be replenished with fresh water. Apart from this, a pool will need little attention for a few years.

Every autumn as the plants die back for their winter rest, the dead foliage and stems should be cut back; if they are not, they will pollute the water as they decay, causing it to turn brown. Cut off dead material cleanly just above water level, not below it, as any hollow stems will become filled with water, and this can cause the crown of the plant to rot. If any leaves from deciduous trees find their way into the water during the autumn they, too, should be removed immediately.

Pygmy water lilies could be damaged by severe frosts, so if you feel they are at risk remove them to a tub in a frost-free but cool greenhouse for the winter; this is easily done if they are growing in aquatic baskets.

A small electric pool heater placed in the water during the winter will help to prevent the water freezing solid during severe weather.

It is not necessary to empty and clean out a pool each spring. A healthy-looking pool should be left undisturbed. However, marginal plants will need to be lifted, divided and replanted every two or three years in mid- to late spring as they start to become congested. The technique is the same as for border perennials – each clump should be split into a number of portions, discarding the old declining center part and saving the young outer portions for replanting. Replant the divisions immediately – do not allow them to dry out.

Miniature water lilies can be left undisturbed for four or five years, when they may then need lifting and dividing in mid- or late spring. Discard the old central crown and retain the outer portions.

Submerged oxygenators may need surplus growth thinned out each spring to prevent congestion. Every two or three years lift them completely, divide, and replant.

When a pool no longer seems as clean as it was, then that is the time to empty it completely, scrub it out and replant with freshly divided plants. Again the best time for a complete clean-out is mid- to late spring.

In summer dead flower heads should be removed from plants so that they don't fall into the water and foul it. Also, do not allow plants to set seeds since this only exhausts them. Plants should be fed each spring, unless they are being lifted and divided, by inserting a perforated sachet of aquatic plant fertilizer into the soil next to each plant. The fertilizer will slowly release nutrients during the course of the growing season.

CONTAINERS IN LARGE WATER DISPLAYS

As one of the basic needs of life, water has an almost magnetic attraction to all living things. Huge waterfalls, cascades, and fountains have for centuries formed magnificent central features in many a grand garden. Yet even in the smallest garden it is quite possible to experience the magical effects of water. Reflected images or the cool and refreshing feel of water are just two experiences offered.

Some plants are particularly fond of water and flourish when their roots are waterlogged – a characteristic that can be put to good use in the container garden.

A simple water feature accompanied by some well-chosen plants will enrich virtually any garden, whatever its size.

ABOVE *An ornamental birdbath is the dominant feature in this raised water garden. White-flowered arum lilies thrive with their "feet" in water, while ivy softens the hard stone.*

RIGHT *Water creates a refreshing centerpiece to this split-level paved area. Container-grown plants such as white* Astilbe *provide a "splash" of color, while the grasses are a perfect complement to the brickwork.*

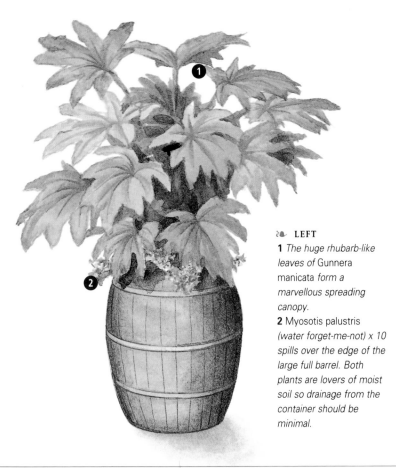

LEFT
1 *The huge rhubarb-like leaves of* Gunnera manicata *form a marvellous spreading canopy.*
2 Myosotis palustris *(water forget-me-not) x 10 spills over the edge of the large full barrel. Both plants are lovers of moist soil so drainage from the container should be minimal.*

ABOVE *Ingredients for a 16in (40cm) half-barrel. Other sedges could be used.*
1 Carex oshimensis *"Evergold"*
2 Iris laevigata *"Variegata"*
3 Nymphaea pygmaea *"Alba" (miniature water lily)*
4 Myosotis palustris *(water forget-me-not).*

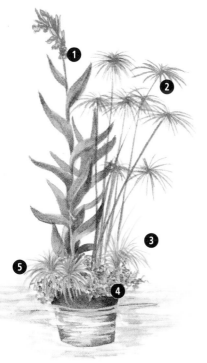

🌿 **LEFT** *For standing in margins of a larger water feature such as a pond. Ingredients for a 20in (50cm) pot. Again, other sedges could be used if these were not available.*
1 Canna x generalis *(Indian shot)*
2 Cyperus alternifolius *(umbrella plant)*
3 Carex elata *"Aurea" x 2*
4 Myosotis palustris *(water forget-me-not) x 5*
5 Carex oshimensis *"Evergold" x 3*

🌿 **LEFT** Passiflora caerulea *(blue passion flower) twines around a pink-flowered* Camellia. *The flowers of both plants resemble water lilies when floated on the water of the adjacent stone pool.*

ATTRACTING WILDLIFE

Water is vital to the survival of all living things, plants and animals alike. A small water feature is therefore the ideal center-piece for an area aimed at attracting birds, butterflies and bees. The color, movement, and sound of these creatures introduces an extra dimension to any garden. A good choice of plants is important. Many fruit- and berry-bearing plants are particularly attractive to birds, while plants whose flowers produce copious nectar entice birds, butterflies, and bees. Seed and fruit trays are an additional attraction for birds. Endeavor to maintain a water supply, especially in very hot or very cold conditions, as the birds will come to rely on it. Position wildlife containers carefully to provide good growing conditions for the plants, and to allow them to be viewed clearly from window or garden.

🐦 **BELOW** *The stone bath acts as a center-piece for a collection of plants selected to attract butterflies, birds, and bees over a long period. This design, shown in autumn, creates a relaxed and peaceful atmosphere. Ingredients:*
1 *weeping* Malus *(crab apple)*
2 Sorbus aria *"Lutescens" (whitebeam)*
3 Ilex *"Handsworth New Silver" (silver holly)*
5 Aucuba japonica *"Crotonifolia"*

6 Hebe franciscana *x "Blue Gem"*
7 Hebe *"La Seduisante"*
8 *blue-violet* Aster amellus *(Michaelmas daisy)*
9 Mahonia aquifolium *(Oregon grape)*
10 Pyracantha angustifolia *(firethorn)*
11 *prostrate* Cotoneaster
12 Ribes uva-crispa *(gooseberry)*
13 Pyracantha atalantioides *(firethorn)*
14 Lonicera periclymenum *(common honeysuckle)*

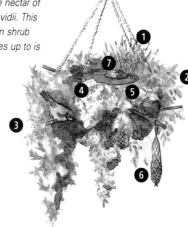

LEFT *Small tortoiseshell butterflies feast on the nectar of Buddleia davidii. This easily grown shrub certainly lives up to is reputation.*

ABOVE *This 16in (40cm) hanging basket, customized for wildlife, is especially useful where space is limited. Shown in early summer.*
Ingredients:
1 *Lavandula stoechas* (French lavender)
2 *Fragaria vesca "Semperflorens"* (alpine strawberry) x 5

3 prostrate *Cotoneaster*
4 *Alyssum maritimum* (sweet alyssum) x 10
5 *Iberis sempervirens* (evergreen candytuft) x 2
6 *Hedera helix "Glacier"* (silver variegated ivy)
7 A dish of water.

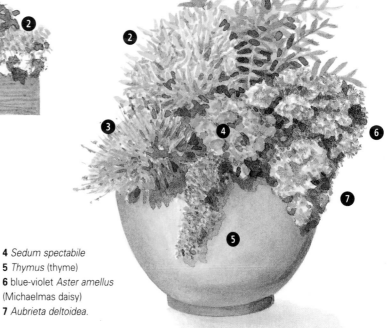

ABOVE *This simple combination is attractive to both insects and humans alike. Ingredients for a 36in (90cm) trough:*
1 *Lantana camara* x3
2 *Tagetes 'Starfire Mixed'* x 15
3 *Alyssum maritimum* (sweet alyssum) x 15.

RIGHT *A design to attract these useful insects over a long period with a succession of nectar-filled blossom. Ingredients for a 28in (70cm) pot:*
1 *Mahonia "Charity"*
2 Lilac *Hebe*
3 *Lavandula stoechas* (French lavender)

4 *Sedum spectabile*
5 *Thymus* (thyme)
6 blue-violet *Aster amellus* (Michaelmas daisy)
7 *Aubrieta deltoidea*.

CHAPTER FIVE

KITCHEN
CONTAINER
GARDENS

Containers can give small gardens the extra space they need for growing fruits and vegetables. If edible plants are chosen carefully for their size, cultural needs, and appearance, they can bring both decoration and harvest to the patio. Many fruit trees are quite ornamental, especially when in blossom and when they are bearing their fruits. And the more attractive-looking vegetables certainly do not seem out of place on a patio. Most herbs are compact, pretty plants that look quite at home in containers.

PATIO FRUITS

Many fruit trees can be grown in containers. Wherever possible choose dwarf trees. Varieties are budded or grafted by nurserymen on to special dwarfing rootstocks that keep the trees small and compact. Make sure you check which rootstocks the trees have been grafted on to when buying – ask for ones suitable for container growing.

Apples and pears – These most popular fruits are available on dwarfing rootstocks. Buy them as dwarf bush or dwarf pyramid trees. The former has a rounded, bushy shape and the latter is pyramid-shaped.

With apples and pears one needs to grow several cultivars together to ensure cross pollination and therefore good crops of fruits. The cultivars must all flower at the same time and they should be compatible – that is, capable of fertilizing each other. Garden centres and specialist fruit suppliers will advise on the best cultivars to grow together.

Cherries – Not so long ago cherries were not grown by many amateur gardeners because they grew into such large trees. Now, however, cherries are obtainable on dwarfing rootstocks and can be grown as dwarf bush or dwarf pyramid trees in containers. As you will probably need only one tree, buy a self-fertile cultivar that does not need to be cross-pollinated.

Plums – At one time these, too, were only available as standard-sized trees, but like cherries they can now be grown as dwarf trees. A self-fertile cultivar on a dwarfing rootstock may be grown as a dwarf bush or dwarf pyramid tree.

Peaches, nectarines – Both of these (a nectarine is simply a smooth-skinned form of the peach) will grow in containers, so long as you get dwarf bush trees. Only one tree of each need be grown, as cross-pollination is not required. However, bear in mind that peaches and nectarines flower early in the year before pollinating insects are around and therefore the flowers have to be pollinated by hand.

This is quite easily accomplished with the aid of a soft artist's paintbrush. Gently dab the center of each flower in turn with the brush so that you transfer pollen from one to another.

Figs – These are very decorative trees, with their large leaves that create a rather exotic atmosphere. When grown naturally they make large specimens, but by restricting the roots in a container they can be kept as small bush trees. Unless they are being grown in a frost-free climate, figs should be removed into a frost-free yet cool greenhouse or conservatory over winter to prevent developing fruits from being damaged or killed by frost.

🍃 **ABOVE** *The satisfaction of growing your own fruit and vegetables comes in being able to pick and eat them at exactly the right moment. Citrus fruits make very handsome tub plants and if you live in a frost-free climate they can be left outside all year round; otherwise give them glass protection over the winter. Some varieties of citrus have variegated foliage.*

Citrus fruits – The same routine applies to citrus fruits, which also make very handsome tub plants when they can be grown as dwarf pyramid or dwarf bush trees. If you are lucky enough to live in a frost-free climate, they can remain outside all year round; otherwise give them glass protection over winter. The most popular citrus fruits for tub culture are oranges, such as the sweet orange (*Citrus sinensis*) and the Seville orange (*Citrus aurantium*). These are also among the hardiest of the citrus fruits.

Grapes – Dessert grapes grow remarkably well in containers and can be trained to various forms. Possibly the most convenient form for containers is the standard (trained to look like a tree), which consists of a single stem, at the top of which new growth that carries the fruit. In early winter every year all these shoots are pruned back on each. (This is called spur pruning.) In cool, temperate climates dessert grapes are best grown in a cool greenhouse or conservatory all year round. But in warmer climates with frost-free winters they can remain outside throughout the year.

CONTAINERS AND PLANTING

Fruit trees look particularly attractive if they are grown in decorative containers. Whatever is used, a diameter and depth of 18–24in (45–60cm) is recommended. Square wooden planters make very attractive containers for fruits, especially if they are painted to match the house. Large terra-cotta pots in plain or ornate styles are also nice. Modern circular concrete tubs would be suitable for a contemporary setting.

However, young fruit trees should not be planted directly in large tubs, but rather started off in 12in (30cm) pots and gradually moved into larger containers. All containers should have a 1–2in (2.5–5cm) layer of pebbles in the bottom to ensure good drainage. This can be covered with a thin layer of rough peat or leaf mold before adding the soil.

Planting and potting can be carried out in late autumn. Fruit trees are best grown in a potting soil containing loam, peat, and sand.

🍂 **ABOVE** *Apples and pears on dwarfing rootstocks make ideal tub plants for a sunny patio. Several different cultivars are needed to ensure cross-pollination of the flowers. Pruning can be a skilled and time-consuming task.*

🍂 **RIGHT** *Blueberries, a recent idea for tub-grown fruits, need acid or lime-free peaty soil, plenty of moisture and may be grown in sun or partial shade. The plants need minimum pruning and their fruits nature from late summer onward.*

 LEFT *The Seville orange (Citrus aurantium) is one of the hardiest of the citrus fruits yet needs wintering in a cool greenhouse or conservatory in climates subject to hard frosts. It thrives in a large tub. Here it is being grown as bush trees.*

This is much heavier than, say, all-peat potting soil and therefore is better able to hold the trees securely. Also, there is less likelihood of the trees being blown over during windy weather. Work the soil thoroughly between the rootball and the side of the container and firm it well. Remember to leave a space of at least 1in (2.5cm) between the soil surface and the rim of the container to allow room for watering.

The following pages give tips about upkeep of the plants.

FRUIT IN
DECORATIVE CONTAINERS

The thought of picking and biting into a juicy home grown peach is ecstasy for many gardeners. If it were only that simple – fruit probably requires more time, effort, and knowledge than any other type of gardening, but consequently it can be also one of the most rewarding.

It is advisable to grow only a single fruit plant in a container, as additional plants would compete for food and water. Therefore the designs below demonstrate the various shapes and forms in which a range of fruits can be grown. There is more than one way of training each type, so choose the method most suited to the situation.

There are many factors to consider when buying a fruit tree, so it is advisable to consult the fruit expert at the nursery or garden centre. A poor choice initially is certain to lead to problems and frustration later on.

It is only fair to point out that a great commitment is required from the fruit gardener, but time and patience will bring success and great satisfaction.

🐞 **RIGHT** *This delicious-looking apple superbly demonstrates how fruit can be successfully grown in containers.*

1 Fan-trained nectarine *(Prunus persica)*
A method ideally suited to growing this sun-loving fruit against a wall, although most fruit will benefit from the shelter afforded by such a position. As well as improving the flavor of peaches, apricots, and pears, their early blossom will be protected from crop-depleting frosts in cooler areas as the wall acts as a storage heater giving off warmth accumulated during the day during the night.

2 Standard gooseberry *(Ribes uva-crispa)* *This method of training is particularly suited to this thorny subject for the container is easily accessible for watering, weeding and feeding.*

3 Triple-cordon redcurrant *(Ribes rubrum)* *Triple cordon refers to the three vertical growths; double and single cordons are also popular. This method allows intensive production in a small area. Apples, pears, gooseberries, cherries and plums can be grown this way.*

4 Bush blueberry *(Vaccinium corymbosum)* *This up and coming fruit is related to the rhododendron, the bush shape being its normal habit of growth. Most soft fruit will assume a bush form if left unattended although correct pruning will lead to greater productivity.*

5 Espalier pear *(Pyrus)* *Along with cordons this is one of the classic forms of training fruit. Unlike cordons the growth is horizontal although the principles involved in training and pruning are the same; so too are the types of fruit suited to this method (see Triple-cordon redcurrant).*

For best results fruit trees need plenty of sun and shelter from winds. The soil should never be allowed to dry out, otherwise this will adversely affect development of the fruits.

Trees should not be allowed to carry excessively heavy crops, as this results in a much smaller crop the following year. If necessary, thin out the young fruits at an early stage of their development.

Fruit trees also need annual pruning, but this is quite a complex subject and varies according to the type of fruit and the form in which the tree is grown. So for full details of pruning, and indeed other routine tasks such as fruit thinning, it is advisable to study a book on fruit growing. Regular spraying to control the numerous fruit pests and diseases may also be required, and again, such information will be found in a specialized book.

Each year in late autumn, mature, established fruit trees should be repotted to replace the soil, which by then will be deteriorating in quality.

6 Dwarf peach *(Prunus persica) These specially bred peach varieties are not quite as flavorsome as the standard types, but offer an option for growing in very small areas and have lovely double rose-red or white flowers. Dwarf nectarines are also available.*

7 Bush apple *(Malus) Apples are also available as dwarfs, in this case the flavor and quality are not sacrificed as the best varieties are grafted onto a dwarfing rootstock, such as M9 or M27.*

8 "Stepover" apple *(Malus) Using a dwarfing rootstock, apple trees are particularly suited to this form. Branches are trained horizontally as near to the ground as possible.*

9 Alpine strawberries *(Fragaria vesca "Semperflorens") These will fruit over a long period when grown in a window box. They are at a convenient height to be picked and eaten fresh.*

10 Grape vine *(Vitis) Reveling in a sunny position a vine can be left to its own devices, but is less productive than if pruned and trained correctly when it can fruit prolifically. Kiwi fruit (Actinidia chinensis) requires similar conditions but detests an exposed site.*

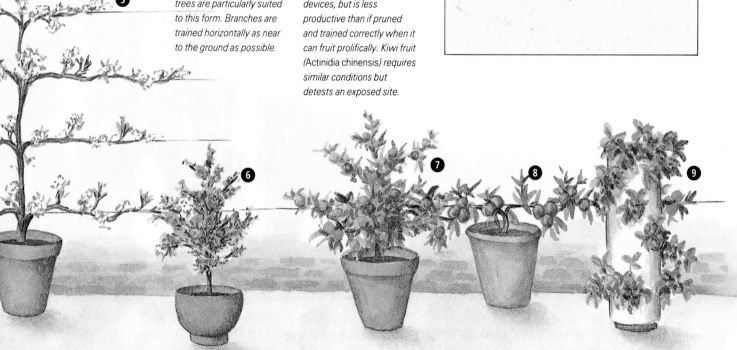

PLANTING A STRAWBERRY BARREL

🌿 **ABOVE** *Ready-made strawberry pots in various designs and materials are available and ideal for mini-patios. Every two or three years all plants need replacing with young ones, which are more fruitful.*

Strawberries take up a large amount of ground if planted in rows or beds in the traditional way. To economize on space and create a striking addition to the patio, balcony, or roof garden, grow them in a strawberry barrel. The best time to plant strawberries is late summer, when they will start cropping the following year.

A large wooden barrel will hold a lot of plants because they are planted in holes in the sides as well as in the top. Drill 2in (5cm) diameter holes in the side of the barrel, about 8in (20cm) apart each way and in a staggered pattern.

Make sure the barrel has some drainage holes in the base and then place a 1–2in (2.5–5cm) layer of pebbles in the bottom to help with drainage. Cover this with a thin layer of coarse peat or leaf mold. Strawberries can be grown in all-peat

potting soil or in a loam, peat, and sand mix. Push the roots of the strawberry plants through the holes as the barrel is being filled with soil. Finish off with about three plants in the top.

Should you not wish to make your own container, you'll be happy to know that there are ready-made strawberry pots available. These are generally terra-cotta containers with holes in the sides. They are lovely when all planted up, but they do not hold as many plants as a large wooden barrel and they dry out quicker.

The soil for strawberries should be kept steadily moist and the plants fed regularly in spring and summer with a liquid fertilizer. In areas prone to frost make sure the flowers are protected; cover the container at night with fine-mesh plastic windbreak netting.

PATIO VEGETABLES

Vegetables can be grown in conventional pots, tubs, barrels, and troughs, which should be at least 12in (30cm) in diameter and depth, or better, 18–24in (45–60cm) wide and deep. They should be filled with an all-peat potting soil. But perhaps the most convenient way to grow vegetables on a patio, balcony, or apartment roof is to plant them in growing bags. These are purely utility containers consisting of a plastic bag about 4ft (1.2m) in length and 12in (30cm) wide, filled with potting soil, generally an all-peat type.

Growing bags are used only for one season, for instance, for a crop of tomatoes, or a succession of several shorter-term crops like radishes. Holes are cut in the tops of the bags for planting or sowing.

Most vegetables like plenty of sun, so choose a sunny part of the patio for them. This is especially important with tender kinds like tomatoes, sweet peppers, and eggplant, all of which also need sheltered conditions.

Some of the taller vegetables will need staking, such as tall tomato cultivars and climbing green and runner beans. You cannot insert canes into growing bags, so other methods of support have to be used. For instance, the bags could be positioned in front of a wall clad with trellis. The plants can then be tied to this, or allowed to twine through it. You can buy growing-bag crop supports for tomatoes and similar plants in the form of a framework made from plastic-coated steel. These have "feet" over which a growing bag is placed to anchor the framework. A similar support could easily be made at home by any handyperson.

WHAT TO GROW

Tomatoes – These are the obvious choice for patio growing bags and other containers. Choose cultivars intended for outdoor growing, either tall kinds, or dwarf bush tomatoes that do not need staking. Tomatoes are raised from seed indoors during early spring and planted out only when all danger of frost is over, in late spring or early summer.

A growing bag will comfortably hold three tomato plants: four generally leads to overcrowding as the plants grow.

Sweet peppers, eggplant – Provided you live in an area with warm or hot summers capsicums, or sweet peppers, and eggplants, will crop well outdoors. There will not be much success with these in areas that have cool summers or in unsheltered sites; there, plants are best grown under glass. Sweet peppers and eggplant are raised and grown in the same way as tomatoes.

Beans – Among pod-bearing vegetables, climbing green beans grow well in containers. They produce heavier crops than dwarf beans, so are more worthwhile. Being tender, they will not tolerate frost. Sow seeds directly in the containers between late spring and mid-summer, spacing them 4–6in (10–15cm) apart.

Runner beans can also be recommended for growing bags, and other containers, and they are highly attractive when in flower. Some cultivars have scarlet flowers, while others are pink or white. Like climbing beans they are frost-tender, but seeds can be sown in the containers outdoors during late spring or early summer. Space seeds 6in (15cm) apart.

ABOVE *French beans grow well in containers and crop during summer. Out of choice, grow climbing cultivars rather than dwarf beans (shown here) as they produce heavier crops.*

A novelty vegetable whose pods are also eaten whole is the asparagus pea (*Lotus edulis*). It has a low, rather sprawling habit and produces masses of very attractive deep red flowers that are followed by angular pods that should be picked when young and tender. Plants are frost-tender. Sow directly in containers during late spring, spacing the seeds 8in (20cm) apart each way.

Radish – Small salad crops are, of course, ideal for containers. For instance, radishes can be sown in succession at two-week intervals throughout spring and summer. Sow thinly and keep well watered for rapid growth.

Beets – Tiny beets can be grown for salads, choosing early round-rooted cultivars and pulling them when young. Sow direct in containers during the spring and thin seedlings to 4in (10cm) apart each way.

Lettuce – Choose some of the more ornamental kinds for the patio, such as non-hearting cultivars, with their deeply cut, frilly leaves (the leaves are picked individually as needed) and red lettuces. Aim for four or five plants per growing bag. Seeds can be sown direct during spring or raised in a greenhouse in pots and planted out when large enough.

Carrots – Young early carrots are suitable for growing bags and other containers. Successional sowings can be made from early spring to late summer. Sow very thinly to avoid the necessity of thinning, which is a fiddly process, and pull them when young and tender.

🌸 **ABOVE** *Growing bags are ideal containers for peas. This tall cultivar will crop heavily during summer from a spring sowing. The plants are well supported by means of proprietary growing-bag crop supports and wooden trellis panels.*

Peas – You obviously cannot grow many peas in containers, so choose the most productive kinds, especially snow pea, or edible-podded, peas. With these there is no wastage; the pods are gathered when young and cooked and eaten whole. Peas are hardy and can be sown in early or mid-spring, spacing the seeds about 2in (5cm) apart each way.

🌸 **LEFT** *Roundrooted cultivars of beets are ideal for salads. They are among the easiest root vegetables to grow and should be harvested while young and tender.*

Winter cress (*Barbarea vulgaris*) – This salad green is good for salads and sandwiches and is easily grown in containers. You can sow right in the bag or other container during early or mid-spring, with additional sowings in summer. If you want a winter harvest, sow again in early autumn. It is important to cover late sowings with cloches or some other form of frost protection. Thin seedlings to about 6in (15cm) apart and keep plants constantly moist. This quick-growing and prolific plant is also a good choice for getting young children interested in gardening. They will also be good at reminding you to water "their" crop.

Zucchini – Zucchini, or courgettes as they are known in France and Britain, are very productive vegetables. They are essentially squashes, the fruits being picked when only 3–4in (8–10cm) in length. Choose bush cultivars rather than trailing kinds. Bear in mind that zucchini are frost-tender. Sow direct during late spring, or raise plants in pots under heated glass, sowing in mid- to late spring and planting out when danger of frost is over. Remember that zucchini are very productive, so two plants will be adequate for a growing bag, setting one at each end.

&. **ABOVE** *Zucchini are popular and very productive vegetables and therefore well worth growing on a patio. Choose bush cultivars rather than trailing kinds. A yellow-fruited cultivar is shown here.*

VEGETABLES ON SHOW

Limited space is no excuse for not growing edible crops. Here are some attractive ideas that can be adapted to suit your own requirements, ranging from small pots, to a large raised bed.

To maximize on available space it is advisable to choose varieties which can be harvested over as long a period as possible. For instance, a winter cabbage will occupy a large space over a long period, whereas a zucchini plant will yield heavily over four months.

While herbs virtually look after themselves, the successful vegetable gardener must be prepared to supply ample water and feed, undertake pest control, and work to a program of successional planting, in order to give continuity of cropping.

🦋 **BELOW** *Originally grown as an ornamental, runner beans (Phaseolus coccineus) are very productive over a long season. Some kinds are particularly attractive in flower. A free-standing 24in (60cm) pot with four support canes makes an attractive feature.*

🦋 **LEFT** *Runner beans (Phaseolus coccineus) trained up a trellis or similar support, will screen an unsightly area, wall or fence. Sow three seeds per cane and thin to leave the strongest plant.*

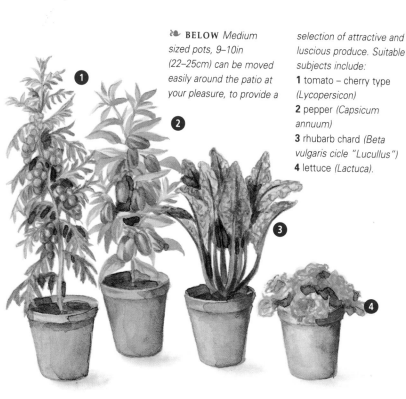

🐦 **BELOW** *Medium sized pots, 9–10in (22–25cm) can be moved easily around the patio at your pleasure, to provide a* selection of attractive and luscious produce. Suitable subjects include:
1 tomato – cherry type *(Lycopersicon)*
2 pepper *(Capsicum annuum)*
3 rhubarb chard *(Beta vulgaris cicle "Lucullus")*
4 lettuce *(Lactuca)*.

🐦 **ABOVE** *A series of small, preferably matching, pots 6–8in (15–20cm) makes an unusually appetizing entrance to a home.* Suitable subjects include: bush tomato *(Lycopersicon)*, radish *(Raphanus)*, chives *(Allium schoenoprasum)*, and lettuce *(Lactuca)*.

🐦 **ABOVE** *A 14in (35cm) basket will supply fresh herbs from spring to autumn and looks effective.*
1 chives *(Allium schoenoprasum)* x 3
2 trailing rosemary *(Rosmarinus officinalis "Prostratus")*
3 Spearmint *(Mentha spicata)*
4 thyme *(Thymus)* x 2
5 parsley *(Petroselinum crispum)*

🐦 **RIGHT** *(left) Some vegetables and herbs are particularly showy as pot-grown specimens.*
1 Fennel *(Foeniculum Vulgare)* grown in a 15in (38cm) pot gives a lovely feathery texture – green – and bronze-leaved kinds are available
2 tuberous-rooted vegetables such as the Jerusalem artichoke *(Helianthus tuberosus)* do well in large pots. Some dwarf varieties can also provide a bright display of flowers at no extra cost. Given frost protection, a good early crop of new potatoes *(Solanum tuberosum)* can be achieved.

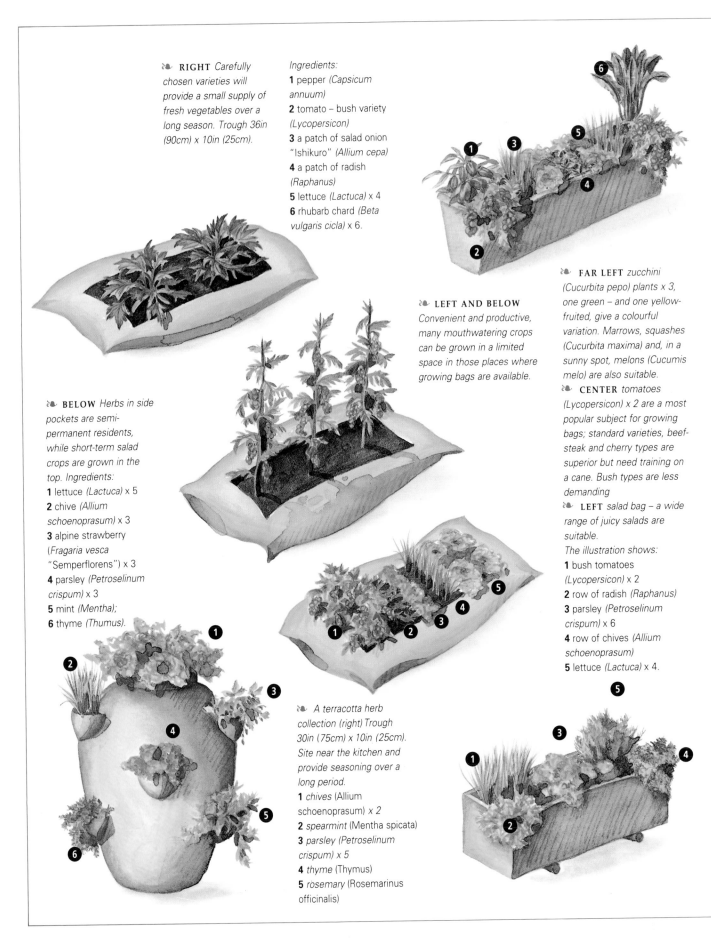

RIGHT *Carefully chosen varieties will provide a small supply of fresh vegetables over a long season. Trough 36in (90cm) x 10in (25cm).*

Ingredients:
1 pepper *(Capsicum annuum)*
2 tomato – bush variety *(Lycopersicon)*
3 a patch of salad onion "Ishikuro" *(Allium cepa)*
4 a patch of radish *(Raphanus)*
5 lettuce *(Lactuca)* x 4
6 rhubarb chard *(Beta vulgaris cicla)* x 6.

LEFT AND BELOW *Convenient and productive, many mouthwatering crops can be grown in a limited space in those places where growing bags are available.*

BELOW *Herbs in side pockets are semi-permanent residents, while short-term salad crops are grown in the top. Ingredients:*
1 lettuce *(Lactuca)* x 5
2 chive *(Allium schoenoprasum)* x 3
3 alpine strawberry *(Fragaria vesca "Semperflorens")* x 3
4 parsley *(Petroselinum crispum)* x 3
5 mint *(Mentha)*;
6 thyme *(Thumus).*

FAR LEFT *zucchini (Cucurbita pepo) plants x 3, one green – and one yellow-fruited, give a colourful variation. Marrows, squashes (Cucurbita maxima) and, in a sunny spot, melons (Cucumis melo) are also suitable.*

CENTER *tomatoes (Lycopersicon) x 2 are a most popular subject for growing bags; standard varieties, beef-steak and cherry types are superior but need training on a cane. Bush types are less demanding*

LEFT *salad bag – a wide range of juicy salads are suitable.*
The illustration shows:
1 bush tomatoes *(Lycopersicon)* x 2
2 row of radish *(Raphanus)*
3 parsley *(Petroselinum crispum)* x 6
4 row of chives *(Allium schoenoprasum)*
5 lettuce *(Lactuca)* x 4.

A terracotta herb collection (right) Trough 30in (75cm) x 10in (25cm). Site near the kitchen and provide seasoning over a long period.
1 chives *(Allium schoenoprasum)* x 2
2 spearmint *(Mentha spicata)*
3 parsley *(Petroselinum crispum)* x 5
4 thyme *(Thymus)*
5 rosemary *(Rosemarinus officinalis)*

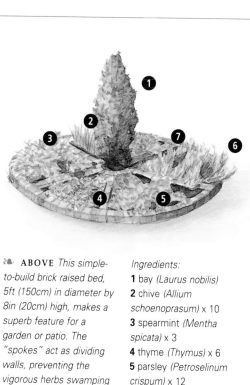

🍃 **BELOW** *The culinary way to add a touch of elegance to a garden or patio. Bay trees (Laurus nobilis) are available in many interesting shapes, excellent as focal points* or in pairs to highlight entrances. Other herbs can provide a softening effect to the container. Shown here:
1 thyme *(Thymus)*
2 lavender *(Lavandula).*

🍃 **ABOVE** *This simple-to-build brick raised bed, 5ft (150cm) in diameter by 8in (20cm) high, makes a superb feature for a garden or patio. The "spokes" act as dividing walls, preventing the vigorous herbs swamping the more delicate.*

Ingredients:
1 bay *(Laurus nobilis)*
2 chive *(Allium schoenoprasum)* x 10
3 spearmint *(Mentha spicata)* x 3
4 thyme *(Thymus)* x 6
5 parsley *(Petroselinum crispum)* x 12
6 prostrate rosemary *(Rosmarinus officinalis "Prostratus")* x 3
7 apple mint *(Mentha suaveolens)* x 3.

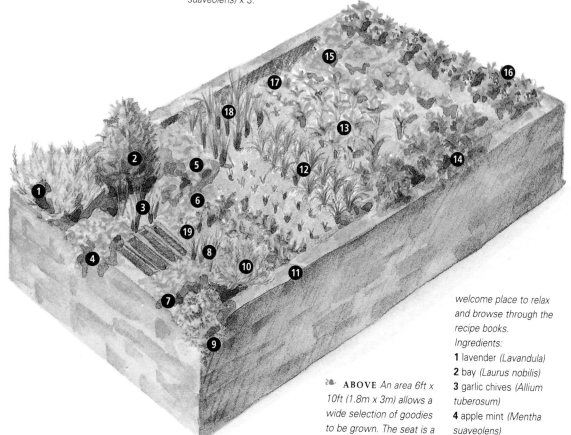

🍃 **ABOVE** *An area 6ft x 10ft (1.8m x 3m) allows a wide selection of goodies to be grown. The seat is a welcome place to relax and browse through the recipe books.*
Ingredients:
1 lavender *(Lavandula)*
2 bay *(Laurus nobilis)*
3 garlic chives *(Allium tuberosum)*
4 apple mint *(Mentha suaveolens)*
5 parsley *(Petroselinum crispum)*
6 sweet basil *(Ocimum)*
7 mint *(Mentha)*
8 chives *(Allium schoenoprasum)*
9 thyme *(Thymus)*
10 rosemary *(Rosmarinus)*
11 kohlrabi *(Brassica oleracea Gongylodes group)*, in a block
12 carrot *(Daucus carota)*
13 Silver beet *(Swiss chard, Beta vulgaris cicla)*
14 tomato – bush type *(Lycopersicon)*
15 lettuce *(Lactuca)*
16 strawberry *(Fragaria)*
17 radish *(Raphanus sativus)*
18 Japanese onions *(Allium "Ishikuro")*
19 pak choi *(Brassica chinensis).*

RAILROAD TIES

Wooden railroad ties are ideal for low raised beds. They are strong, long-lasting, and a particularly "sympathetic" material for the garden. They also have a bold profile that can help to give a garden a strength of line and design that is sometimes lacking with other materials. There are two problems: weight and availability (there are firms that supply new ties); ask the local station where to obtain old ties in your area.

It takes at least two strong people to lift a railroad tie, and additional help is advisable. As they are also difficult to cut, it is best to use whole ties whenever possible. Some will probably have to be sawn, but working to halves and using a chain saw will minimize the effort.

Because of their weight, beds up to three ties high are unlikely to require additional securing or staking, and they can simply be stacked. Stagger the joints at the corners, so that they form a bond (see illustration). Deeper beds should have strong iron stakes driven either side of the sleepers, to reduce the risk of them toppling.

On a sloping site, ties can be used to form a stepped or tiered effect.

LOG BEDS

Logs create a very different atmosphere from railroad ties. They are much more rustic and informal in appearance, and lack the crisp, neat outline of ties. They generally have to be higher to look right (beds just a couple of logs high generally appear insignificant), and the rather bulky appearance means they are more

ABOVE By using railroad ties as part of the paving pattern as well as for the raised beds, a more integrated garden design can be achieved. If the area is small, like this, the raised beds should not be too high – otherwise the sense of scale and proportion will be destroyed.

WOODEN RAISED VEGETABLE BEDS

Wood is a material very much at home in the garden and old railroad ties, rustic logs, and planking can all be used to make raised beds. Building a raised vegetable bed in wood is a rewarding way to add a note of permanence to a garden, but don't let it overwhelm.

RIGHT Stack the ties so that they are bonded at the ends, like brickwork. Using full or half-length ties will save alot of hard physical work and make bonding easy.

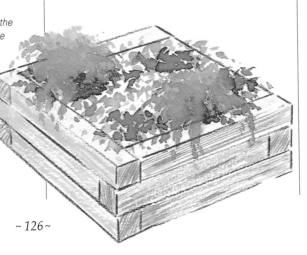

suitable for shrubs and bold herbaceous plants than the less substantial seasonal bedding. They generally look best in an informal garden, perhaps with woodland in the background.

Use logs of even thickness about 6–8in (15–20cm) in diameter.

Different joints produce different visual effects. The halved joints at the ends create a neat, more formal finish that makes the bed more functional with attention focused on the plants. They are also easy to make with a chain saw. The notched and overlapped joints (see illustration left) make the log bed itself a key feature.

There will probably be some gaps where the logs do not meet exactly. This problem is easily overcome by lining the sides with thick polythene, butyl pond liner, or even old carpet. Always ensure that there is free drainage at the base.

Various pressure-treated pine log kits are available for making raised beds.

A BED FOR VEGETABLES

A raised vegetable bed like the one shown is a very simple do-it-yourself project and provides a better place to grow vegetables on a patio than scattered about in containers.

A softwood can be used to keep the cost down, but it should be thoroughly treated with a preservative, preferably pressure-treated before purchase. Rough-sawn timber will be slightly less expensive than planed and finished timber.

Planks 9in × 1in (230mm × 25mm) or 12in × 1in (300mm × 25mm) are suitable for the sides (the larger size is more appropriate for a large bed), with 3in × 3in (75mm × 75mm) timber for the corners, supports, and anchor posts.

If the bed is to stand on a solid base, make the corner supports the same depth as the planks, but if possible extend them by about 12in (30cm) to anchor them in the ground as shown. Nail the planks to the corner supports. If the bed is more than about 6ft long, insert additional anchor blocks along the sides and secure with nails.

ABOVE *Raised beds of limited height can be made from quite modest timbers. The supporting pegs (below) should, however, be well secured in the ground to withstand the pressures created within the bed.*

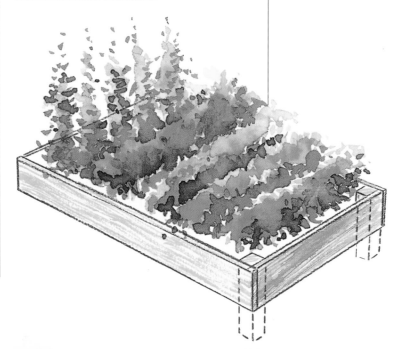

☙ **RIGHT** (below) The subtle variations of leaf color and shape, with the occasional flower, give this arrangment its own particular charm.

☙ **ABOVE** Another use for a "strawberry barrel" – a home for a collection of herbs. Avoid planting mint as it will quickly take over the barrel.

☙ **RIGHT** Window boxes also make excellent containers for herbs. Pick off leaves or young shoots as needed.

CONTAINER HERBS

Culinary herbs can be grown in ornamental terra-cotta pots or troughs and need a very well-drained soil and plenty of sun. Several small herbs could be planted in a large pot or trough. A group of containers planted with herbs could make quite an attractive feature on a patio. And the cook in the family will welcome the easy access to a range of useful kinds of herbs.

There is a very wide range of culinary herbs available but people find the following the most popular and the most useful.

ANNUALS

Several popular herbs are annuals and need to be sown afresh each year. Included here is parsley (*Petroselinum crispum*), which is sown direct in early or mid-spring. Seeds are slow to germinate. Sometimes this plant will reseed itself. The tender basil (*Ocimum basilicum*) is sown outdoors during late spring, as is coriander (*Coriandrum sativum*) and dill (*Anethum graveolens*). Chervil (*Anthriscus cerefolium*) is a hardy biennial grown as an annual and can be sown from late winter to mid-autumn in succession. Sweet marjoram (*Origanum majorana*) is a half-hardy annual sown during late spring.

PERENNIALS

Of the permanent perennial herbs suitable for growing in containers, common mint (*Mentha spicata*) must be the most popular. It is rampant, so it is best grown in a container on its own. Keep the soil moist. Mint can be grown in shade if desired. Lift and divide every two years in early spring. Sage (*Salvia officinalis*) is a popular perennial, as is thyme (*Thymus vulgaris*). Chives (*Allium schoenoprasum*) form neat clumps of foliage that have an oniony flavor. Lovely lilac-colored flowers appear in late spring. Plants should be lifted and divided every two years in early spring. Pot marjoram (*Origanum onites*) is another useful culinary herb, as is wild marjoram or oregano (*Origanum vulgare*).

A tall herb for the back of a group is fennel (*Foeniculum vulgare*), which has beautiful feathery foliage. It bears yellow flowers in summer and would not look out of place in a group of ornamental plants.

Two very popular herbs are tall shrubs and should have containers to themselves. One is the sweet bay (*Laurus nobilis*), with large, evergreen, lance-shaped leaves that are aromatic. It responds well to regular clipping so it can be grown as a trained specimen, such as a pyramid or mop-headed standard. It is on the tender side, so in areas with hard winters it is best wintered in a greenhouse.

The evergreen rosemary (*Rosemarinus officinalis*) has small, aromatic leaves and in spring produces tubular, lipped, mauve flowers. This is another rather tender shrub and needs winter protection under glass in cold areas. It is very decorative and could be included in a group of ornamental shrubs if desired.

Do not subject herbs to hard freezing. Winter in a cool greenhouse if necessary.

ABOVE Mixed herbs look especially attractive in terra-cotta pots and make a pleasing as well as practical patio feature. They need plenty of sun.

LEFT Variegated and purple sages growing with marjoram – surely as pleasing as any flower display.

~ 129~

SCENT THROUGH THE OPEN DOOR

The presence of scent in the garden is often undervalued. Many plants can offer at least a hint of perfume, but carefully chosen varieties will provide some delightful effects. The scent of spring hyacinths wafting in through an open window, or the fragrance of summer honeysuckle as the front door opens are always welcome, if often unexpected.

❧ Flowers are by no means the only purveyors of scent. The leaves of numerous plants provide some most pleasant aromas when crushed between the fingers or merely brushed against. Some plants have a scent so strong it fills a garden on a still evening, but most perfumes are intimate and are best when encountered at close quarters. For this reason scented plants should be thoughtfully positioned, so that they can be easily and regularly appreciated. The window sill, the patio, and, in particular, the entrance area are prime sites.

❧ **RIGHT** *The central lily flanked by pot-grown Daturas creates a deliciously fragrant combination. The aroma of the silver-leaved Helichrysum italicum (curry plant) will also enrich the evening air.*

❧ Our designs show some seasonal schemes and some which will provide different scents over most of the year. Scented leaves and flowers can be combined effectively and the addition of some bright and colorful bedding plants will complete the effect.

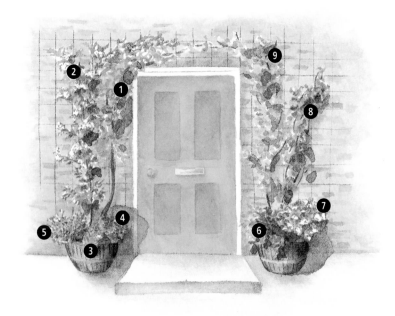

❧ **LEFT** *This design will provide a succession of different and very desirable scents intermittently throughout the year. Illustrated at its peak in spring to summer. Ingredients for a pair of 20in (50cm) tubs:*
1 *Lonicera periclymenum* (common honeysuckle)
2 *Jasminum polyanthum*
3 *Thymus x citriodorus "Aureus"* (golden lemon-scented thyme)
4 *Daphne odora "Aureo-marginata"*
5 *Lavandula angustifolia "Munstead"* (lavender)
6 *Mahonia aquifolium* (Oregon grape)
7 *Choisya ternata* (Mexican orange blossom)
8 *Trachelospermum jasminoides* (star jasmine)
9 *Rose* "Alberic Barbier"
Bulbs: *Hyacinthus, Narcissus "Cheerfulness," Convallaria majalis* (lily of the valley).

FAR LEFT A scented pot for late spring *Ingredients for an 18in (45cm) pot:*

1 Narcissus white *"Cheerfulness"* × 12

2 Myosotis alpestris *(forget-me-not)* × 5

3 Convallaria majalis *(lily of the valley)*

4 Primula × polyantha *(polyanthus)* × 5

5 Dianthus barbatus *"Giant Auricula Eyed" (sweet William)* × 5

6 Cheiranthus cheiri *(wallflower)* × 5.

CENTRE Scent at a pinch *A group of plants with aromatic leaves. Ingredients for a 20in (50cm) pot:*

7 Thuya plicata *"Zebrina"*

8 Salvia rutilans *(pineapple sage)*

9 Thymus × citriodorus *"Aureus" (golden lemon-scented thyme)*

10 Lavendula stoechas *(French lavender)*

11 Pelargonium tomentosum *(peppermint geranium)*

12 Eucalyptus citriodora *(lemon-scented gum).*

BOTTOM Summer scents *Ingredients for a 15in (38cm) pot:*

13 Lantana camara

14 Heliotropium arborescens *(cherry pie)* × 3

15 Alyssum maritimum × 10

16 *pink, scented* Verbena × 3

17 Matthiola bicornis *(night-scented stock), sow a few pinches of seed after pot is planted.*

BOTTOM RIGHT Sweet summer perfumes *Ingredients for a 20in (50cm) pot:*

18 Hedychium gardnerianum *(ginger lily)*

19 Lilium auratum

20 *white* Nicotiana alata *(tobacco plant)* × 5

21 Heliotropium arborescents *(cherry pie)* × 3

22 Lathyrus odoratus *"Bijou Mixed" (sweet pea)* 5.

LEFT Heady evening scent *Ingredients for a 24in (60cm) pot:*

23 *peach-flowered* Datura *will fill the evening air with its delicious fragrance*

24 Alyssum *"Wonderland"* × 12 *adds color and daytime scent at low level.*

CHAPTER SIX

THE PRACTICALITIES

Thomas Edison once described invention as "one percent inspiration and ninety-nine percent perspiration." Most good gardeners would like to think that their work put more stress on the inspiration, but they recognize the need to plan on a daily, seasonal, and annual basis. The same diligence and patience also pay dividends when gardening with containers or window boxes. Every stage of container gardening benefits from planning beforehand, and watchfulness is the only real way of dealing with pests, diseases, or the threat posed by the weather.

It cannot be denied that growing plants in containers is quite labor-intensive, particularly during warm weather when they will need a lot of watering. Then there is feeding of plants (needed more often than plants growing in the garden), changing potting soil, moving plants into larger containers, the pruning of some permanent plants (although the same plants in the garden would also require this), and protection during the winter if you live in an area subject to severe frosts.

All of these tasks can become labors of love or necessary chores, depending on your point of view or the amount of free time you might have. The main thing to remember is that planning, pruning, repotting, and general maintenance are the cornerstones of good container gardening. This chapter provides the advice you will need to set about looking after your current displays and setting the stage for next year's. You might become ambitious and try building a larger container – a wooden container that acts almost as a flower bed but has the attractions of a container. Container plants can also be "put to work," hiding ugly features outside or creating privacy in the house.

Vigilance is essential with container gardening, because the comparatively small amount of soil must nourish your displays over a season or perhaps right through the winter. Pests and diseases – or the two weeks you are away on vacation – can quickly take their toll on plants growing in a confined space. It is important that these plants have the best nourishment and that pests and weeds are denied a foothold.

Pruning and deadheading are essential for appearances and for the well-being of the plants themselves. They are especially important features of container gardening, since the containers are drawing attention to the plants within them.

Likewise, winter preparations are a bit more involved with containers since those plants that are not winter-hardy must be protected at the first threat of frost. Water displays and window boxes merit special attention. Suggestions for winter – and the

whole gardening year – appear in the "Year-Round Action Plan" at the end of this chapter (pages 156–157).

CHOOSING COMPOST

Along with adequate feeding and watering, a suitable compost is crucial for success with container plants. It is tempting to use garden soil, especially for large containers and for shrubs and small trees that normally fend for themselves perfectly adequately in garden soil, but plants in containers are handicapped. Their roots cannot explore new ground freely

ABOVE An attractive greenhouse can become a summer feature in its own right. It "pays its keep" during the colder weather, when container plants can be overwintered away from the threat of frost.

for nutrients, and they cannot tap reservoirs of water normally held in the lower depths of the topsoil, and perhaps even subsoil. Plants grown close together in a window box or hanging basket, for example, are in the same competition for nutrients and moisture as they would be if surrounded by weeds in the ground. In the case of hanging baskets, weight is also an important consideration. So choosing the right compost is vitally important.

LOAM COMPOSTS

Loam-based composts are preferable wherever weight is not a problem. They are easy to keep evenly moist, they have a better natural reserve of nutrients and, for large plants with a lot of heavy top growth, they provide better anchorage and stability. The main problem is one of quality, as loam (the basic ingredient) is variable. Loam composts made to the British John Innes formula are generally used to provide some standardization. The potting composts are graded 1 to 3, depending on the amount of fertilizer they contain. For most containers No. 2 is ideal, but for very vigorous plants (such as tomatoes) or for large shrubs and trees No. 3 is appropriate. In other countries proprietary loam-based potting composts are often graded by strength and those with the greatest supply of nutrients, or with slow-release fertilizers, are the best choice for permanent plants.

PEAT COMPOSTS

Peat-based composts have two major advantages: they are clean and easy to use, and they are light. The downside is that once they dry out rewetting them thoroughly is difficult (the water tends to run through them), and nutrients are quickly exhausted.

Peat composts made early headway with the UC (University of California) range of composts, but various formulations are used everywhere now. Proprietary brands vary considerably but it is best to assume that all plants in peat-based composts require feeding after about a month, unless slow-release fertilizers are present.

Peat-based composts are not generally suitable for containers planted with large perennial plants, partly because of their inability to sustain good growth over a long period but also because loam provides more stability for large bushy plants.

ALTERNATIVES TO PEAT

Concerns about the depletion of peat reserves and the effect of peat extraction on wildlife and the landscape, has encouraged the development of alternatives for soil-less composts. Some of these are based on chipped and treated bark and on products such as coconut fiber. As these become more widely available and more experience is gained with them for a wide range of plants, their strengths and weaknesses will become apparent. They are, however, worth using for seasonal plants.

CONTAINER COMPOSTS

There are proprietary container composts, developed primarily for hanging baskets and window boxes. These may be loam-based, but they usually have a high proportion of peat or other light products to reduce the weight. They may also have water-retaining products (see Compost Additives) and slow-release fertilizers to maintain steady growth.

It is worth experimenting with several different brands of compost to see which one suits the kind of plants that you grow.

COMPOST ADDITIVES

Some compost additives to improve structure or increase water holding capacity, such as vermiculite and perlite, have been used for many years to retain water and open up a heavy soil. Now the super-absorbent polymers are becoming popular. These crystals or gels can absorb and hold water which is then available to the plants for a longer period – theoretically a great advantage for plants in containers. They are available from garden centers so you can mix them into your own compost. However, although possibly beneficial, frequent watering on warm days will still be necessary, so the solution to low-maintenance containers is more likely to lie with some form of automatic watering (see pages 136–137).

COMPOST FOR LIME-HATERS

Lime-hating plants require an acid compost. Although peat is acid, peat composts normally have neutralizing agents added, which makes them unsuitable for those plants that prefer an acid compost, such as *Rhododendron*. Both peat-based and loam-based composts are available for these plants, and are generally labeled as such.

The homemade organic compost described below can be made suitable for lime-haters by omitting the lime and ensuring that the loam used is acid or neutral.

🍃 **ABOVE** *Hydrangeas react to the amount of lime in the soil by changing the color of their flowers. On alkaline soils blue varieties may turn pink; for good blues, use an acid compost.*

🍃 **RIGHT** *Some plants, such as rhododendrons, will not thrive in an alkaline (chalky) soil, and a container may be ideal if the garden soil is not sufficiently acid.*

COMPOSTS

🍃 **Compost decisions** *These are just some of the compost types that can be used for containers:* **1** *loam based (John Innes),* **2** *organic compost based on animal manure,* **3** *coconut-fibre compost,* **4** *hanging-basket compost,* **5** *peat-based compost,* **6** *loam-based container compost.*

ORGANIC COMPOSTS

Organic composts are available in various mixes and for various plants to use in pots or containers. These are based on products such as peat and cow manure or composted bark and animal manures. They will produce good results but are often more expensive than conventional composts.

An effective homemade organic compost for containers can be made as follows. Mix 7 parts of loam, 3 parts of well-rotted garden compost, manure or leaf mold (or sphagnum moss), and 2 parts of coarse grit. Add 1oz (30g) of garden lime and 5oz (150g) of blood, fish and bone meal to each 2-gallon (9-liter) bucketful of the above mixture, and mix.

Bear in mind that plants grown in organic composts still require feeding.

WATERING

Regular watering is essential for plants in window boxes. The small amount of soil in the boxes dries out quickly, so watering will be a regular task in warm weather, when some containers may need checking twice a day. Do not neglect to check them regularly in cooler weather, too, even in winter, when the soil can still dry out, albeit more slowly.

The best way to judge when plants need water is to stick your finger into the soil; if the soil feels dry an inch or two below the surface it is time to water. Do not wait until your plants droop or wilt before watering them. Wilting means that plants are suffering water

stress, and although watering may revive them, water-stressed plants grow slowly and produce fewer flowers.

Overwatering creates as many problems for plants as underwatering. When the soil is constantly soggy, plant roots cannot get air (which is essential) and the plants can literally suffocate. Soggy soil also encourages diseases. If your plants develop yellow leaves and drop a lot of leaves, they are probably getting too much water.

When you water your plants, do it gently but thoroughly. Water the soil at the base of the plants; don't just sprinkle the plants from above. Continue watering until excess water drips from the drainage holes in the bottom of the window box. It is important that the soil be moistened all the way through, so all the roots receive water.

To make sure that the spray of water is not too strong, forcing soil out of the container or damaging leaves, either use a watering can or a hosepipe fitted with a trigger-operated watering lance or nozzle.

Some gardeners like to mist their plants to allow the leaves to absorb moisture directly. If you decide to mist your plants, do so early in the morning or late in the afternoon. Avoid getting water on foliage at midday when the sun is at its hottest (the water droplets act like little lenses, focusing the sunlight and causing burning of plant leaves). Also avoid misting at night; when foliage remains wet in still night air, fungus pathogens may attack it.

If you are growing lime-hating plants such as rhododendrons, remember that some tap water may contain lime. The plants will object to this and their leaves will turn yellow. Instead collect and use rainwater.

To ensure your plants receive enough water while you are away, consider a temporary automatic watering system – say a drip system consisting of a main garden hose fitted with thin tubes that continuously drip water slowly into the containers. This system can be run from a water reservoir (such as a small tank raised above the ground) or from the main water supply via a header tank with a control valve.

RIGHT *Watering is a regular task in warm weather when some containers may need checking twice a day. Water in the evening or early in the morning, and give enough water so that it starts to trickle out of the bottom of the container.*

LESSENING THE BURDEN

Slow-release fertilizers can relieve the burden of regular feeding, but watering is a regular and for much of the year a *daily* chore that has to be faced up to as the one major negative aspect of container gardening. Only automatic watering systems can ease the commitment required. A single day of neglect can ruin a hanging basket, and even some of the tougher shrubs in tubs can suffer permanent damage if neglected during a summer holiday.

🐦 Automatic or semi-automatic watering systems are generally designed for greenhouses, where plants are conveniently grouped together; containers in the garden are often placed around the garden making it difficult, both practically and visually, to hide their "mechanics." A combination approach is likely to be the most satisfactory solution for most gardeners.

GARDEN HOSES

A hose that has to be wound and unwound by hand, and fitted to the tap each time, either won't be used regularly or will be left lying around the garden. Investing in a through-feed hose-reel permanently fitted to an outside tap is one of the best investments for anyone with a lot of containers to water. Fold-flat hoses are easy to put away, but less convenient than through-feed reels and some tend to kink badly if taken round a sharp corner.

🐦 Hoses are particularly useful for watering hanging baskets, but the main disadvantage is that a forceful jet of water will tend to wash the compost away from the roots. Hose-end attachments often make the spray even more forceful, or alternatively produce a fine spray that makes it difficult to judge when enough water has been applied. Either use the hose with the tap turned on just sufficiently to produce a trickle, or hold a piece of rag over the end to break the force of the jet and prevent damage to delicate plants.

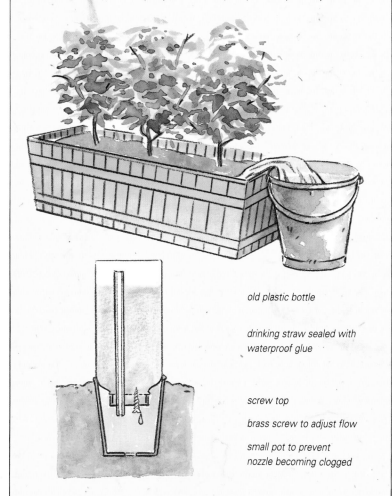

VACATION CARE

The best form of vacation care is a helpful neighbor. Failing that, try arranging a capillary system as shown or try making a simple temporary drip feed from an old plastic bottle (see illustration). Lift down baskets and treat like other containers. If possible move them to a shady spot.

Various wicks can be improvized, but the best is a piece of capillary matting of the kind sold for greenhouse watering. Cut a broad strip from it and bury one end deeply into the compost, making sure the other end goes right to the base of the water container (weight it down with a brick).

The bottle system illustrated should prevent a container drying out completely for a couple of days.

old plastic bottle

drinking straw sealed with waterproof glue

screw top

brass screw to adjust flow

small pot to prevent nozzle becoming clogged

🐦 **LEFT** Through-feed hose reel *A very convenient way to water several containers. The hose is easily rewound after use.*

🐦 **RIGHT** Fold-flat hose reel *Useful for storing conveniently, but not as easy to use as a normal through-feed hose and reel. Some of these hoses are liable to kink.*

For shrub tubs and troughs at ground level a large garden watering can is the most practical – there are fewer trips between tap and containers, and it is not necessary to lift the heavy can to any significant height. For window boxes and other raised containers, a smaller greenhouse watering can with a long spout is more practical, even though the capacity is less. Always use a rose on the can, even though it takes longer to water. This will minimize water runoff while at the same time protecting delicate stems and foliage.

KEEP WITHIN THE LAW

In some areas, a back siphonage protection device must be fitted to an automatic watering system if it uses a hose connected to the mains water supply – in fact it is a requirement for all garden hoses. Failure to do so may be a health risk, or illegal, so contact the local water authority for advice.

SELF-WATERING CONTAINERS

Although intended for indoor use, these provide the real solution for a balcony or veranda. The plastic containers are attractive, and even in the summer they are unlikely to need topping up more frequently than once a week. Plants generally thrive in this kind of container.

BASKET WATERERS

Proprietary basket waterers, based on a plastic bottle and tube with a curved end, which work by squeezing the bottle, are convenient for one or two baskets but time-consuming if you have a lot of baskets.

Some compression sprayers have an extension tube with a curved end, designed to make basket watering relatively simple. These work well, but again may be inconvenient if there are many baskets.

AUTOMATIC SYSTEMS

These are most justified when there are a lot of containers in a relatively small area that can be fed from one source. Drip-feed systems are effective for a long row of hanging baskets; for instance, as the supply tubing can be run along the support unobtrusively with small drip tubes leading down into the baskets. They are also useful for tubs and large pots if the supply tubing can be laid unobtrusively.

With a drip-feed system simply turn on the faucet and leave until the containers have received enough water or, better still, use in conjunction with a timer faucet to make the system automatic – even while on vacation.

Systems like this require regular checking. Nozzles can become blocked, and if they are adjustable it may be necessary to vary the flow occasionally.

There are various devices for automatically watering. Well-directed spray systems may be quite useful to water an entire potted vegetable garden, including tubs of cucumbers and zucchini.

RISE AND FALL OF A HANGING BASKET

A pulley-type fixing, made specifically for hanging baskets, will enable a basket to be lowered easily to a convenient height to water with an ordinary watering can. They can be suspended on a bracket or fastened directly to a beam. Such a fixing has many other advantages. For example, it allows gardeners with disabilities a chance to gain extra height for their displays. It also offers a handy way of hoisting baskets out of the reach of young children.

FERTILIZING AND FEEDING

Anyone who has seen trials of fed and unfed, but otherwise identical, containers, and especially those with limited compost capacity such as hanging baskets, will have no doubt about the importance of feeding. Quite simply it will make the difference between a poor, mediocre display and one that is first-rate with lush, healthy growth. The effects of feeding are most dramatic with seasonal plants in peat-based and peat-alternative composts, but even trees and shrubs in loam-based composts will benefit. Container-grown plants need more feeding than plants in the garden, for nutrients are washed out of the potting soil during watering. However, only feed plants while they are growing – in the spring and summer, never in autumn and winter. And do not apply extra fertilizer until plants are well established because new potting soil contains fertilizer, and this should be used up first before you start feeding.

Plants in window boxes will exhaust the nutrients in the soil after about a month. To keep them growing well, you will need to fertilize regularly after the plants are established. Wait until the plants have been growing for several weeks before you feed them; fertilizing young plants too soon overstimulates them, resulting in rapid, weak growth and generally poor performance. Overfeeding plants at any stage of their development will have the same effect.

Almost all plants in containers require feeding at some stage but how soon depends very much on the compost. Some peat-based composts, for instance, contain fertilizers which produce very good growth initially but become exhausted rapidly; others contain plant foods that produce less lush growth early on but sustained growth for longer. Increasingly, slow-release and controlled-release fertilizers are being used in composts, and these may sustain good growth for many months without additional feeding.

🐚 **BOTTOM LEFT** *This example of a well-watered and well-fed container shows vigorous and healthy plants that are clearly growing well. The Sedum planted around the base of the Clematis shows how containers can be made much more interesting with thoughtful planting.*

🐚 **BELOW** *Most composts will have started to run out of nutrients long before the plants have filled the basket as well as these violas. The use of slow-release fertilizers, or regular feeding, is crucial to maintain this kind of display.*

FEEDING TREES AND SHRUBS

Trees and shrubs that are in a container for many years require feeding at least a couple of times a year, preferably with a slow-release fertilizer. If this is not possible use a balanced general purpose fertilizer for the flower garden, either a powder or granules.

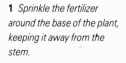

1 Sprinkle the fertilizer around the base of the plant, keeping it away from the stem.

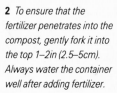

2 To ensure that the fertilizer penetrates into the compost, gently fork it into the top 1–2in (2.5–5cm). Always water the container well after adding fertilizer.

You cannot tell how well a particular compost is going to perform simply by looking at it. It make sense to find one you like, to learn by observation when its food reserves are likely to become exhausted, and then use it regularly. The performance of different feeds can also produce strikingly different results – it's worth trying several, on a range of containers, to see which gives the best results (but bear in mind that some fertilizers may be better for particular plants). When you water the plants, the fertilizer will be dissolved and then absorbed by the roots. Be cautious when applying granular fertilizers because they can burn plant roots if they come in direct contact with them. Apply the fertilizers when soil is moist so that they will dissolve quickly and harmlessly.

WHEN TO FEED

The early stages of starvation are not always obvious unless controls are grown alongside. Plants that just don't seem to be growing well or that seem a bit "slow" could be due to the weather, or an unsuitable position. With seasonal summer plants, however, the signs are frequently very obvious even within weeks of planting (some may have become starved in their pots or seed trays beforehand), with small, yellowish leaves and stunted growth. This demands immediate feeding.

FOLIAR FEEDS

Some liquid feeds can also be used as foliar feeds (check the label), and applying them to the foliage means they are taken in by the plant more rapidly. They are easy to use, and nutrients become available to plants immediately. The fertilizer is diluted with water and then applied to the soil surface or sprayed onto the plants' leaves, a process known as foliar feeding. Foliar feeding produces very quick results, but does not last as long as fertilizers applied to soil, so it should be applied more often. Some products sold specifically as foliar feeds contain other substances to stimulate plant growth, and are intended to revive sickly plants. Never apply a foliar feed while plants are in strong sunlight.

LIQUID FEEDING

Liquid feeds are generally cheaper than other plant foods, and some provided as powders to dissolve in water are particularly economic. However, having to water them *regularly* is time-consuming if there are a lot of containers and obtaining the correct dilution is an additional chore. Liquid feeding is the best option if you use liquid feeds in other parts of the garden or in the greenhouse, and want to keep costs low.

PELLETS, STICKS, AND TABLETS

There are several products designed to be pushed into the compost, near the plants' roots. The number required depends on the size of the container, but the manufacturer's instructions make this clear. Whether they come in tablet form or as sticks, they must be pushed into the soil with a pencil or piece of dowel.

The products vary widely, not only in formulation – some are intended primarily for flowering plants, others are aimed at foliage plants – but also in how long they last. Some might require replenishing after a few weeks, others after months, though all are applied much less frequently than liquid feeds. They are the best choice if you are not able to incorporate slow-release fertilizers when planting yet find liquid feeding a bit of a chore to do regularly. Keep a supply of these products handy if you are planning a vacation during the growing season.

ORGANIC FERTILIZERS

Both liquid and solid fertilizers are available in various synthetic and organic formulations. Organic gardeners used to have to apply several different materials to get a balanced plant food (such as dried blood for nitrogen, bonemeal or rock phosphate for phosphorus, granite dust or greensand for potassium), but in recent years organic fertilizer blends have become available. Good organic liquid fertilizers are fish emulsion and seaweed concentrates. Several brands of powdered organic fertilizers of different nutrient formulations with varying strenths are also available.

SLOW-RELEASE FERTILIZERS

These are generally mixed in with the compost, but can be added later when they should be gently worked into the top half-inch or so of the compost. Some are in sachets that are put under the rootball when planting.

Slow-release fertilizers are available from garden centers, who can advise on brand names. Not all work in the same way, though for use in the spring all are satisfactory. Some release nutrients slowly over a period of many months; others only release them when the temperature is warm (useful for autumn application, as it is undesirable to stimulate growth during the winter). In general, one application will provide seasonal plants with nutrients for the whole season – ideal if you want to forget about feeding.

WHEN NOT TO FEED

A few plants are best grown without too much fertilizer. Some annuals, such as Tropaeolum (nasturtiums), may produce so much foliage that the flowers are hidden if too much nitrogen is given. Some Pelargoniums are special cases, best grown to discourage too much leafy growth – the famous Balkon or Cascade Pelargoniums (the same plants, just different names in different countries) have to be planted close together and grown with little fertilizer if they are to flower freely.

Alpines and cacti also require less feeding than, say, summer bedding plants.

Autumn-planted bulbs will not require fertilizer, unless part of a permanent planting and then in spring and not autumn. Avoid stimulating any plant into growth as the cold weather approaches.

SLOW-RELEASE SACHETS

Some slow-release fertilizers come in sachets to put beneath the plant. Because these can only be used at planting time, they are only suitable for seasonal plants. Make the planting hole, then drop the sachet into the bottom before planting. The number required will depend on the size of the container so follow the manufacturer's advice.

CONTAINER CARE

Once a year it is worth checking all containers to see whether they require any maintenance. Although gardeners go to great lengths to make a new "stone" container look old, a grubby one may cease to be attractive, and damaged containers can be given a new lease of life with simple repairs.

Cleaning should never be drastic. Plastics and ceramic tiles can be wiped over with a normal nonabrasive kitchen cleaner, but concrete and reconstituted stone containers are best scrubbed with a hard-bristled brush using a mild detergent; if stubborn stains remain try a little diluted bleach on the area.

The white deposit that sometimes forms on terra cotta is often acceptable, but to remove it try scrubbing the affected area with a strong solution of vinegar.

Wooden containers can be brightened simply by scrubbing with soapy water; periodically they will need painting again – if the finish is natural wood, use a wood preservative, perhaps one containing a stain.

Repairs can be made to concrete and reconstituted stone containers that have been slightly damaged. If a piece of decoration has been knocked off, it can usually be stuck back satisfactorily with a two-part epoxy resin (make sure both surfaces are clean).

If a concrete container is chipped in an inconspicuous place, try using a fine concrete mix, first using a PVA adhesive to paint the damaged area to ensure a good bond. Some manufacturers of the more expensive reconstituted stone containers might supply a repair kit.

LEFT *This antiqued lead tank is attractively weathered but it could be quickly neatened up by a scrub with a stiff brush and a strong solution of vinegar.*

PESTS AND OTHER PROBLEMS

Pest and disease control should never be a major problem, and simple precautions should largely eliminate the need for pesticides. Careful choice of plants and varieties, and ensuring that the plants are well fed and not overcrowded, go a long way to eliminating pests and diseases, but *some* problems will still be encountered.

PRACTICAL PRECAUTIONS

Even gardeners who don't mind using chemical sprays must prefer to minimize their use, if only to save money and time.

Here are simple precautions that make sense whatever your views on pesticides.

🍃 Grow resistant varieties whenever possible. If growing roses, choose those that show a high degree of disease resistance; if growing *Antirrhinum* (snapdragons) in an area where rust is a common problem, grow rust-resistant varieties. If you live in an area where rust is a common problem on *Althaea* (hollyhocks), grow varieties that can be treated as annuals (by not overwintering the plants you reduce the risk of the disease).

🍃 Avoid plants that are known to be particularly susceptible to pests or diseases

WIND SHIELD

Some vulnerable evergreens that are not particularly hardy can be damaged by cold winter winds. A sheet of polyethylene around the sides may offer enough protection.

ORGANIC REMEDIES

If preventative action has not worked and you want to avoid using the more highly developed chemicals, try the following. A soft soap solution should kill most insects on contact but there are insecticidal soaps that have added ingredients to improve the kill of more resistant insects such as whitefly, scale insects and red spider mites (again there must be direct contact with the pest). Derris is popular for controlling crawling pests such as caterpillars, and pyrethrum can be useful against aphids. For fungus diseases Bordeaux Mixture (a copper fungicide) can be tried, and green sulphur is useful against powdery mildew.

unless you are prepared to spray; for example, *Tropaeolum* (nasturtiums) may well attract aphids, particularly blackfly. In your area there may be certain plants that always seem prone to particular pests and diseases. Make a point of eliminating these for a simple but effective control.

🍃 Keep the plants well fed. Healthy plants are more able to resist disease.

🍃 Avoid very overcrowded containers. It is usually possible to ensure a full and well-fitted display while still allowing enough room for air to circulate around the plants. Overcrowding can lead to the rapid spread of both pests and diseases.

🍃 *Observe.* Make a point of checking for early signs of pests and diseases when you water (or make it a specific job once a week). Picking off affected leaves or shoots at the earliest signs of infection or infestation will often eliminate a problem before it spreads. As an additional precaution, carry a small ready-mixed insecticidal "gun." This is not an economic way to treat a widespread infestation, but it is so much more trouble to mix up an insecticide than to give a single squeeze on a trigger that the chances are you won't bother until the population builds up. Using a small amount of insecticide *early* and confining it to the part affected is both economical and environmentally sensible. For aphids there are comparatively safe and "natural" insecticides that you can use.

🍃 **ABOVE** *Plants on the borderline of hardiness can be helped to survive by plunging the pots in the ground and tying straw or dried bracken around them as a protective coat.*

Although there are more potentially harmful insects, diseases and disorders than most gardeners care to think about, just a handful of garden chemicals will control most problems. Often there are alternative forms of control too.

It is most convenient and practical to summarize the problems and the solutions under a few broad headings to cover the major problems likely to be encountered.

Leaf eaters bite holes in leaves or around the edges. These are most likely to be caused by caterpillars (which will probably be visible), or insects such as weevils or earwigs (which will probably be hiding). Dust the area with a contact insecticide.

Slugs and snails can devastate newly planted seedlings or vulnerable foliage plants such as hostas. Snails will be found on the leaves, slugs will usually leave telltale slime trails even if the pests are hiding. Pick off and destroy them and use a slug killer around the base of the plant.

Remember to check the undersides of leaves and the leaf axils (where leaves join the stem) as well as the tops of the leaves when looking for pests.

Sap suckers such as aphids and thrips may cause deformed flowers and shoots, and generally weaken plants. Aphids, the most common problem, are easily seen as small green or black "flies" (though they don't always have wings). Apart

🐌 **ABOVE** This Choisya ternata (Mexican orange blossom) has been damaged by exceptionally cold winds in a severe winter, but it will recover and produce new leaves.

from spoiling and debilitating the plant directly, they may transmit virus diseases. Many common pests, such as aphids, whiteflies, and spider mites, can be washed off plants with a hose if the infestation is not too severe. If water does not remove the pests, spray with an insecticidal soap solution to get rid of them. Insecticidal soap is a very effective pest control, and it is harmless to people and pets. If your windows are open in summer, chemcials sprayed on your plants will drift into your house, so it is best to avoid using these products on window boxes. Some other insecticides to control aphids do not harm beneficial insects. A systemic insecticide is the best solution.

Mildews and molds, rusts and rots cause rotting flowers, fruit and leaves. These and any leaves with brown spots, pimples or blotches are best picked off promptly and burnt. A systemic fungicide such

as benomyl will give some control of most fungus diseases except rust and downy mildew – for these try mancozeb.

Problems in the soil can be caused by various grubs and larvae which eat the roots of plants, or chew at the stem at ground level. If this appears to be a problem, change the container soil and improve growing conditions, although established plants are less likely to be affected.

Pale, yellowish leaves may be due to a nutrient deficiency. If there are no signs of insects (check with a magnifying glass), try feeding the plants with a balanced feed containing trace elements. If this doesn't work, a virus might be the cause.

Viruses could be the cause of stunted plants with mottled or yellowish leaves. They are the most likely cause if a single plant is affected. If there is no other more likely cause, pull up the affected plant and burn.

The weather, in the form of heat, drought, cold winds, and frost, can damage the edges of the leaves on evergreen trees and shrubs which can turn black or brown. New leaves should be unaffected. The new foliage on vulnerable deciduous plants such as *Acer palmatum* (Japanese maples) may shrivel up shortly after they have opened; this can be caused by very cold winds. Very hot sun can also damage the leaves. More protection is the answer.

PRUNING, DEADHEADING, AND WEEDING

Plants in containers need routine care like grooming, pruning, and staking just like any other garden plants, albeit on a more modest scale. This is specially important for containers with perennial plants, though even seasonal plants require some attention. Just keeping the containers looking neat will improve appearances.

Pruning will usually keep shrubs looking attractive. It is as important for shrubs in containers as it is for those in the ground, and should never be neglected. Although many shrubs are pruned in spring, everything depends on the plant concerned (by pruning at the wrong time the season's flowers may be jeopardized). Many permanent ornamental plants like shrubs and climbers do not need any pruning apart from the removal of dead and dying wood. However, there are some that need regular attention, as detailed below.

Heaths and heathers, santolina (cotton lavender), senecios and lavenders – These small shrubs need to have their dead flowers removed. This is quite a simple and quick operation. Trim off the dead flowers immediately after blooms have faded with a pair of sharp garden shears, but do not cut into the wood.

Hydrangeas – Leave on the dead blooms of hydrangeas until the spring in areas subject to frosts, as they help to protect the dormant buds just below.

Carefully cut them off with hand pruners taking care to avoid damaging the new buds.

Rhododendrons – Remove the seed heads as soon as flowering is over. It is not a good idea to allow these to develop, since most people do not save the seed and allowing them to fully develop uses up a lot of the plant's energy which would be better diverted to the production of flower buds for the following year's display. Rhododendron seed heads are easily removed by twisting them off, but take care to avoid damaging the new buds just below them as you do so.

Forsythia – This shrub needs regular pruning immediately after flowering. Left unpruned, forsythia quickly develops a messy, straggly appearance. Cut the old flowered stems back to young shoots lower down and remove some of the oldest woods, while retaining plenty of new or comparatively new growth.

Kerria japonica – This plant and its cultivars are pruned after flowering by cutting back old flowered stems to strong, young shoots lower down. Some thinning out of old shoots may also be required to encourage new growth from ground level.

Roses (Rosa) – Some roses need annual pruning in early spring. Floribundas are pruned first by cutting out all weak and dead growth and then reducing the remaining strong stems to within 8in (20cm) of soil level. Make the cuts just above buds that face outward. The bushes should have an open centre, free from any growth.

LEFT *Floribunda roses need annual pruning in early spring to encourage plenty of young, vigorous flower-producing growth.*

LEFT *A number of plants need to have their dead flowers removed to prevent energy-consuming seed production. Examples are rhododendrons (shown here), roses, heathers and bedding plants.*

With climbing roses you should allow a permanent framework of stems to build up. These will produce side or lateral shoots, which will bear the flowers. Pruning involves cutting back the side shoots to leave only their bases, each with one or two growth buds. If the main stems start to become too tall, then cut out their tips.

Miniature roses do not need regular pruning. Simply remove any dead and dying wood as soon as you notice it.

Sweet bay (Laurus nobilis), holly (Ilex), and box (Buxus sempervirens) – If these plants are grown as clipped specimens they should be trimmed as necessary during the summer to keep them neat.

Box can be trimmed with a pair of sharp garden shears, but the large-leaved sweet bay and hollies are better trimmed with hand pruners to avoid cutting the leaves in half. Cut leaf edges turn brown, creating an unsightly appearance. It can be rather slow and tedious cutting each shoot with hand pruners, but it is well worth the trouble in the long run.

Winter jasmine (Jasminum nudiflorum) – This climber should have some of its oldest and weakest wood cut out completely. Then prune back old flowered shoots to leave only about 3in (8cm) of their base. Prune winter jasmine immediately after flowering.

Summer jasmine (Jasminum officinale) – This is also pruned immediately after flowering. The oldest shoots should be thinned out to prevent congested growth, but do not reduce in length any of the remainder.

Clematis – The large-flowered hybrid clematis need pruning, but the method varies according to type. The hybrids that flower from late spring to mid-summer on wood formed the previous year, like "Lasurstern" and "Nelly Moser," can be left until growth starts to become congested. Then in late winter they can be cut down to within about 3ft (90cm) of soil level. In the spring they will make plenty of new growth.

Those clematis that flower during summer and autumn on the current year's shoots, such as "Jackmanii Superba," should have all their growth cut back to just above soil level in late winter each year. Make the cuts right above strong growth buds. This sounds drastic, but they will make plenty of strong new growth in the spring.

PRUNING HERBACEOUS PERENNIALS

So far this chapter has been discussing the pruning of woody plants such as shrubs and climbers. But herbaceous perennials also need annual attention. In the autumn the top growth dies down and the plants take a rest over winter. The dead growth should be cut down to soil level in the autumn. Evergreen perennials do not die back, but some of the leaves die and these should be removed as necessary.

The foliage of spring-flowering bulbs dies down each year in the summer, at which stage it can be cut off at ground level. On no account cut off bulb foliage before it has completely died down, otherwise you will jeopardize flowering the following year. The plants need this foliage to allow the bulbs to build up and gain strength for flowering again. Without foliage this will not happen and blooms will not be produced. In fact, to help in this building-up process, feed the bulbs with a liquid fertilizer two or three times in the spring after flowering while the foliage is still green.

DEADHEADING

You should regularly remove the dead flower heads of bedding plants, as this encourages more to be produced and therefore extends the flowering period. This is perhaps more important with summer bedding plants, but spring-flowering kinds like polyanthus should be deadheaded, too. Seed production stops plants from producing more blooms, so if you prevent this from happening then the plants will quickly develop more flowers with the view to setting a crop of seeds. Admittedly it can be a tedious job going over the plants with a pair of flower scissors, but it is well worthwhile for the extended display.

Clearly there are some plants, those with masses of small flowers, such as *Lobelia* and *Alyssum*, where deadheading is not practical without a great deal of time and patience.

Some perennials, such as *Aurinia saxatilis* (*Alyssum saxatile*) and *Aubretia*, look tidier, and the plants remain more compact, if trimmed over with shears after flowering.

MULCHES AND DECORATIVE FINISHES

Containers with perennial plants ought to be kept looking fresh, and by topdressing and mulching the plants will benefit too. Remove any existing mulch or decorative finish, such as gravel, along with about 1–2in (2.5–5cm) of compost, without damaging the main roots.

🐾 **ABOVE** *In hot areas some plants in containers, such as lilies, will suffer if the soil heats up too much. The containers may need to be shaded with sun-loving plants but the tops of the plants still enjoy plenty of sun.*

Replace with a layer of fresh compost (this is sometimes called topdressing), and apply a thick layer of pulverized bark, decorative stone chippings or gravel.

WEEDING

If a sterilized loam-based or a peat-based compost has been used, weeds should never be a major problem, but seedlings will appear (sometimes self-sown seedlings of the cultivated plants). Pull them out while still young as they will compete with the cultivated plants for nutrients and moisture.

POTTING AND REPOTTING

Permanent plants like shrubs and trees should not be planted immediately in large containers (unless, that is, you purchase large specimens). Ordinary, small young specimens are better started off in smaller pots and gradually potted into larger sizes (two sizes larger each time) before the pots become packed with roots, until they are large enough for their permanent pots. Moving plants into larger pots like this prevents roots of young plants rotting from large volumes of wet soil around them.

Plants can be potted in early spring just before they come out of dormancy and start into growth again. The technique is as follows: first make sure that the plant's rootball is moist. Ensure the container has drainage

🐾 **BELOW** *When planting several plants together, first fill the container with soil, then make a hole for each one. The design should be well thought out before you plant.*

holes in the base, then spread a layer of pebbles over the bottom for good drainage. Cover this with a thin layer of rough peat or partially rotted leaves. Then put a layer of potting soil over the drainage layer and firm it in place. If you are planting just one plant put it in the centre of the container. (If you are planting several smaller plants, see the alternative method, below.) Adjust the depth of the soil layer if necessary, bearing in mind that when potting is completed there must be a ½–1in (12–25mm) watering space at the top of the pot and that the top of the plant's rootball should be covered with ½in (12mm) of new soil.

Next fill the space between the rootball and the sides of the container with new potting soil, firming it with your fingers as you proceed, only lightly if all-peat, or moderately if it contains loam, peat and sand.

This technique should vary slightly if several plants are to be planted in a container such as bedding plants or small permanent kinds like shrubs or perennials. Prepare the container as described above. Fill it with potting soil and then make individual planting holes. Insert a plant in each and then firm the soil around them.

With either technique, water the plants gently but well to settle them in after planting, using a watering can fitted with a sprinkler.

🌿 **BELOW** *It is best to pot plants just before the present pot becomes packed with roots. Prepare a pot about two sizes larger, putting pebbles in the bottom for drainage. Position the plant centrally on a layer of fresh potting soil well down between rootball and sides of pot.*

REPOTTING

Repotting is a technique used for single permanent plants in containers like trees and shrubs, including fruit trees. It is a means of changing the potting soil without providing a larger container and it applies only to plants in their final, permanent containers. Potting soil has to be changed every so often because it starts to deteriorate in quality and then plants do not grow so well. Drainage and aeration may become poor and plant foods may have been leached out. In these conditions plants make poor or little growth.

How often should one repot permanent plants? Ideally fruit trees, which expend a lot of energy on fruit production, should be repotted each year in late autumn. You need not go to all this trouble with other trees or shrubs quite so often; once every two years should be sufficient. When they are dormant in late autumn is a suitable time for repotting deciduous trees or shrubs, but evergreens are better repotted in mid-spring.

Repotting often involves large containers, so two people may be needed for the operation. Place the container on its side. One person should then firmly tap the rim of the container with a block of wood while the other person gently pulls on the plant. The rootball should then slide out of the container. However, if the rootball sticks, work a long, sharp blade of some kind all around, between the rootball and the side of the container. Then try again to slide out the rootball. Do not risk damaging the rootball by rushing this procedure.

Once the rootball is exposed it should be made smaller by about 2in (5cm) all around to allow space for fresh potting soil. Using a small handfork, tease away some of the old soil all around, including top and bottom. If necessary, some of the roots can be trimmed back by about 2in (5cm) with hand pruners.

Cover the plant's rootball with wet burlap to prevent it drying out while you wash out the container and dry it completely. Then put the plant back in its container and follow the step-by-step instructions on potting, earlier.

TOPDRESSING

In the years between repotting topdress your plants. This involves scraping away about 1in (2.5cm) or more of the old soil from the top of the container and replacing it with fresh potting soil. This is easily and quickly achieved and well worthwhile. Spring is the best time for topdressing.

OTHER SOIL CHANGES

The soil in containers used for temporary bedding plants should be changed every alternate year before it starts to deteriorate too much in quality. Simply remove all the old potting soil (this can be spread on the garden) and drainage material, thoroughly wash the inside to remove all traces of soil, allow it to dry completely, then replace the drainage layer and fill with new potting soil. The soil in hanging baskets and wall pots can be replaced each year in the spring before you plant them.

Groups of small permanent plants in containers, such as dwarf shrubs and perennials, heathers and dwarf conifers are usually left alone until the containers start to get overcrowded. Then the plants can be lifted and planted in the garden. The containers are cleaned, supplied with fresh soil and planted with new, young plants. Bear in mind that some plants can be divided into smaller portions, especially many perennials, so you may not need to replace all the plants with new ones that you removed. The best time for dividing perennials, and indeed for replanting containers, is in early spring.

STAKES AND SUPPORTS

Whenever possible shrubs and small trees should be grown in containers without supports as it is difficult to secure a large stake in a container, it will simply blow over along with the plant in exceptionally severe weather. It is better to encourage a sturdy plant able to bend with the wind to some extent. But a small temporary stake is a sensible precaution for trees until the plant

🍂 **ABOVE** *In the years between repotting, topdress permanent plants by removing the top 1in (2.5cm) layer of soil in the spring and replacing with fresh soil.*

has filled the container with roots and found a firm anchor.

Some bulbs and herbaceous perennials will bend or flop and spoil the display, specially if near a wall or fence where wind hitting the wall is forced back against the plants. Proprietary plant supports can be used for large floppy herbaceous perennials, but for plants like *Narcissus* (daffodils) a few split canes inserted near the edge of the container with cotton stretched between them is generally satisfactory.

One of the best ways of supporting a climber is to fix a wooden trellis to a wall or fence, and stand the container at the base.

Tall vegetable plants in containers definitely need support, especially the tall type of tomatoes (you could grow compact bush varieties instead). It is better to grow them in containers with broad bases.

Runner beans in tubs can be supported with a wigwam of bamboo canes tied at the top. A wide range of compact bush varieties of vegetables have been bred for container growing and these won't require any staking.

SUPPORTS

1 *The most satisfactory support for climbers is a wooden or plastic trellis fixed to the wall. If the container is pushed close enough the plants will climb easily.*

2 *Plants in growing bags are difficult to support because the depth of compost is so shallow. Proprietary growing-bag supports are the best solution.*

3 *Plants that are usually self-supporting but may be blown over by winds if shallowly planted in a container, such as daffodils, are best supported with split canes and twine.*

5 *To produce a wigwam of canes it is best to have plastic holders that secure the canes at the top.*

4 *For tall herbaceous plants, the wire supports sold for use in borders can be used.*

PUTTING CONTAINERS TO WORK

These projects offer some solutions to problems you might face around your property. Containers provide attractive buffers for privacy – or simply hide unsightly walls or building features.

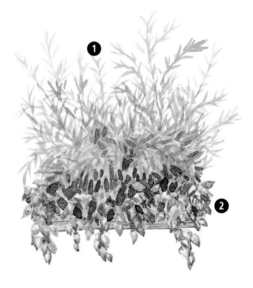

ABOVE *Bamboo curtain. A window box provides some privacy for a large room. Ingredients for a 4ft (1.2m) trough:*

1 *Phyllostachys nigra (bamboo) is sparse enough to allow light into the room x 3*

2 *Hedera helix "Goldheart" (gold-variegated ivy) visually softens the container x 4.*

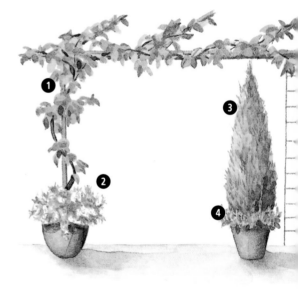

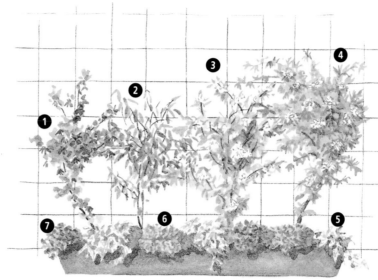

▟ **BELOW**

Plants for a purpose.
1 *Vitis* (Grapevine) spreads over the trellis to provide dappled shade on a hot summer's day
2 *Convolvulus cneorum* x 3 spilling over the edge of the 20in (50cm) pot, is also a sun lover
3 *Juniperus scopolorum* "Skyrocket" forms a strong pillar completing the archway started by the vine. Between them they define the entrance clearly
4 *Diascia cordata* x 5 flow out of the pot
5 *Fremontodendron californicum* makes a floriferous yet open and airy screen
6 *Convolvulus mauritanicus* x 3 has a lax habit and blue flowers which contrast superbly
7 *Hedera helix* "Goldheart" (gold-variegated ivy) forms a visually solid corner to the area while its irregular growth habit "breaks up" the strong outline of the structure.

▟ **ABOVE** *Screening a fence or wall. A run of troughs is planted with climbers which are supported by a wire fence or trelliswork. As climbers are, by nature, sparsely clad at the base, lower growing plants are used to furnish this area. The illustration shows a recently planted scheme during mid-summer. After two more growing seasons this will be a dense wall of intermingled plants.*

Ingredients for a 10ft (3m) set of troughs:
1 *Lonicera x brownii* (scarlet trumpet honeysuckle)
2 *Clematis armandii*
3 *Solanum jasminoides* "Album" (white-flowered potato vine)
4 *Passiflora caerulea* (blue passion flower)
5 *Hedera helix* "Glacier" (silver variegated ivy) x 3
6 *Hebe x franciscana* "Variegata" x 2
7 *Diascia cordata* x 5.

▟ **RIGHT** *A free-standing screen. A large wooden barrel, 32in (80cm) across, with the top removed and a trellis supported by a central post. Ingredients:*
1 *Hedera colchica* "Dentata Variegata" (variegated elephant's ear ivy) x 2
2 *Clematis* "Jackmanii Superba"
3 *Eccremoncarpus scaber* (Chilean glory flower) x 3
4 *Vinca major* "Variegata" (variegated greater periwinkle) x 6
5 *Lonicera japonica* "Aureo-reticulata" (variegated Japanese honeysuckle).

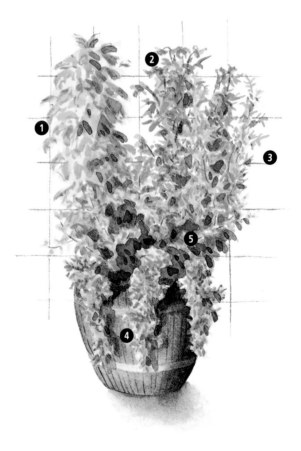

GOING "PERMANENT"

Years of growing in containers might whet your appetite for providing a more permanent setting for your plants. A raised bed is a handy way of combining the handsome look of a container with the scope of a flower bed.

Brick is an ideal material for making raised beds. The units are small enough to enable a wide range of designs to be created in many shapes and sizes, and they are relatively light and easy to handle. Equally important, bricks blend with plants and the muted colors are often less obtrusive than concrete walling blocks.

Although simple rectangular beds are quick and easy to construct, raised beds will make a better feature if they are a little more imaginative. The two types of brick raised bed illustrated here are simple to construct and both make interesting garden features.

Many clever variations can be created by joining a series of rectangles, perhaps at varying heights for extra interest.

INTERLOCKING BOXES

As the plan on this page shows, three simple "boxes" were used to form the brick planter illustrated. By altering the height of each box, even by one or two bricks, the effect is made more interestsing. Experiment with different proportions and sizes, and adjust the height to create more variations. Lay the bricks loosely on the ground initially to gain a better idea of what the design will look like in the garden.

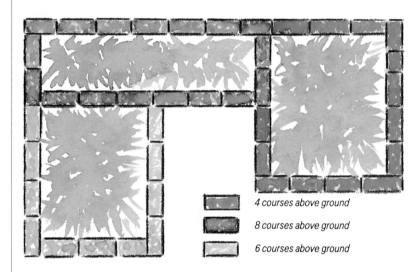

LEFT *Plan on paper. It is always worth drawing out the plan on paper first, as this makes it easier to visualize the proportions of the various boxes and enables the correct number of bricks to be calculated.*

4 courses above ground

8 courses above ground

6 courses above ground

RIGHT *A brick-built raised bed like this is an ideal project for anyone who wishes to acquire simple bricklaying skills. The job can be completed relatively quickly, no complicated bonds are required, the minimum of brick cutting is necessary, and the cost is not prohibitive.*

LEFT *Circular beds
are more complicated to
construct, but well within
the scope of most home
enthusiasts. They can be
planted with a tree in the
center or used for
seasonal bedding or
shrubs – all with equal
success.*

*The illustration shows
how the ground is marked
out to an accurate circle
and the walls constructed
on a concrete footing.*

CIRCULAR BEDS

Once the front row of bricks has been laid,
circular beds are not as difficult to build as
they might appear. First draw a circle of the
required radius using two sticks and a length
of string (see the illustration below). This will
give a reference line on which to lay the bricks
out loose. However, minor adjustments will
probably be necessary to keep cutting and
mortar gaps to a minimum. Then lay the

concrete footing and when that has set lay the
bricks.

To avoid cutting all the bricks, lay whole
bricks with their ends pointing outward – to
create the curve it is necessary to have the
inner ends almost touching and a wider
wedge of mortar facing outward.

Cut bricks in half and use them for the final
row so that the brickwork does not look too
dominant for the size of the bed.

A FRAME OF REFERENCE

BELOW *Mark out a
circle to excavate a
trench.*

*Use a spirit level on a
straight-edge over a series
of pegs to ensure an
accurate level, then fill
with concrete to this level.*

*Use cut bricks for the top
row (an angle grinder can
be used to ensure clean
cuts.*

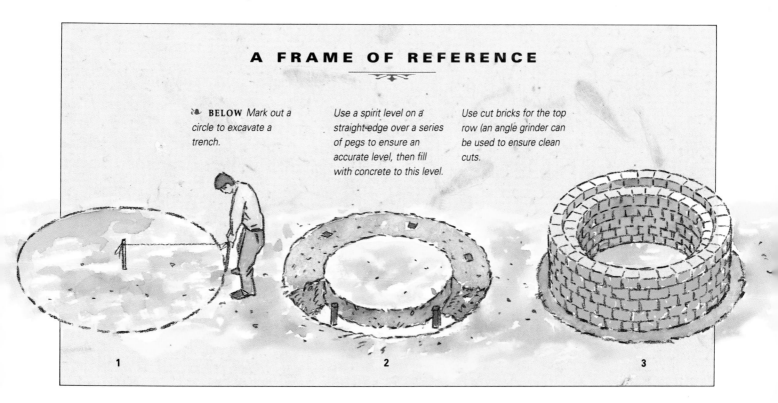

1

2

3

PRACTICAL POINTS

Even low raised beds require a firm and level concrete footing. Lay a concrete foundation strip 6in (15cm) thick and 18in (45cm) wide, ensuring it is level. There should be one course of bricks below ground level, so allow for this when calculating how deep to excavate.

Special quality frostproof bricks should be used for garden walls in cold areas, so always check with the supplier that they are suitable for garden walls, otherwise they may crumble after repeated wetting and freezing.

Insert a layer of damp-proof course material (which comes by the roll), and paint the inside of the raised bed with a bitumen-based waterproof paint, otherwise white deposits may become a problem on the brickwork.

BELOW *The bright green stems of Cornus stolonifera "Flaviramea" add an extra element of display to the garden in winter.*

WINTER PROTECTION

A problem with container growing in areas that experience severe frosts in winter is that the potting soil can freeze solid for prolonged periods. The frost itself will not harm very hardy or tough plants; the problem is rather that it prevents them from absorbing water and therefore the plants could die of drought! One way to prevent this happening is to move the containers into a frost-free yet cool greenhouse or conservatory during severe weather. This will certainly be necessary for less hardy and tender plants that could be damaged or killed by severe frosts.

Tough plants that can be left outside during severe spells could have their containers insulated to help prevent the soil from freezing solid. There are various natural materials one could use, like bracken or straw. The containers should be wrapped with a thick layer of these materials, which can be held in place with wire netting.

Although not aesthetically pleasing, thick wads of newspaper make excellent insulation and can be held in place in the same way. Fiberglass roofing insulation is another material that could be used; again the end justifies the unattractive means.

Another possibility is plunging containers to their rims in the soil in a spare part of the garden. To prevent the ground around them from freezing, mulch with a 6in (15cm) deep layer of bulky organic matter such as peat, leafmold, chipped or pulverized bark, straw, or bracken.

In hot areas it is not frost that is troublesome, it is the sun. Some plants like clematis, camellias, and rhododendrons, and many shade-loving plants, suffer if the soil heats up too much. To help keep temperatures down in containers, shade them as much as possible with growth from other plants. Bushy plants grouped around containers will help to shade them, as will trailing plants cascading over the edge. Or place containers with heat-sensitive plants in more shady conditions where they will not receive the intense midday heat.

PREPARING WINDOW BOXES FOR WINTER

Clean up your window boxes in autumn so they will be ready for planting the following spring. Pull up and discard annuals when the plants stop blooming or are killed by frost. Cut back herbaceous perennials to the ground, and prune or trim woody-stemmed perennials, shrubs, and trees. Move tender perennials and houseplants back indoors before the weather turns cold. Isolate plants coming back indoors from the rest of your houseplants for a few weeks to make sure they are not harbouring pests that could spread to other indoor plants. Lift tuberous begonias, dahlias, and other tender bulbs and store them indoors over the winter.

If you grew geraniums (pelargoniums) in your window boxes, cut back the plants, pot them up, and bring them indoors for the winter. You might also take cuttings and start new plants indoors. Cut back the plants the following spring to encourage new growth when the plants are moved back to the window boxes.

ABOVE *To prevent soil from freezing solid over prolonged periods in winter, which may harm even hardy plants, containers can be moved into a cool conservatory during severe weather. Tender plants in containers will need protecting in the same way, but throughout the winter.*

YEAR-ROUND ACTION PLAN

EARLY SPRING

Brighten winter and spring window boxes and tubs by plunging pots of early bulbs among evergreens. If these have not been grown specially for filling gaps, small pots of bulbs are usually available from garden centers.

Remove winter protection from tender plants in mild areas. In cold areas it may be wise to delay until mid-spring.

Finish planting bare-root trees and shrubs, container-grown plants can be planted at any time.

MID-SPRING

"Instant" spring displays can be achieved by using pot-grown plants from garden centres. Some small spring-flowering plants such as *Bellis perennis* can be bought in pots in garden centers, and together with pot-grown pansies and pot-grown spring bulbs a very attractive display can be created instantly. If planting a window box, knock the plants out of their pots before planting.

Supports for certain plants may be necessary by mid-spring – see *Late Spring* for techniques.

Remove winter protection from tender plants if not already done, but don't expose frost-tender plants at night until all risk of frost has passed in cold areas.

Plant evergreens – this is one of the best times.

LATE SPRING

Get supports into position for summer-flowering border plants and others that need support for the summer before growth becomes too advanced. The plants will grow through and hide the supports.

Putting supports in too early can make the containers look unattractive while the plants are growing.

Apply a balanced fertilizer to trees and shrubs or better still, topdress by removing a few centimetres of compost from the top of the container and replacing it with fresh compost enriched with a little extra fertilizer.

Plant hanging baskets but do not hang them out until danger of frost has passed. If possible keep them in a sheltered place, glasshouse, or shadehouse for a few weeks to become established.

Plant tender vegetables such as runner beans, aucchini, eggplant, capsicums, sweetcorn, cucumbers, and tomatoes.

EARLY SUMMER

Put out hanging baskets and plant out summer annuals. A good guide is when the local parks department plants out its summer flower seedlings. A wide range of seedlings can be bought at local nurseries and garden centres.

MID-SUMMER

Start feeding seasonal displays if a slow-release fertilizer has not been used.

Deadhead and groom plants wherever this is practical.

Sow biennials such as wallflowers and forget-me-nots in a nursery bed.

LATE SUMMER

Continue feeding and deadheading all displays.

Plant autumn-flowering bulbs such as colchicums as soon as they are available. Colchicums are sometimes coming into flower while still in the nursery if you wait a little longer, but it is easier to plant them in containers before the flower shoots have emerged.

EARLY AUTUMN

Take cuttings of pelargoniums (geraniums) if you have somewhere that is warm, shady and protected from wind to grow them on. Coarse river sand is a good medium in which to root the cuttings.

Continue feeding those plants that still have several weeks of display left.

Take in tender plants, such as house or greenhouse plants that have been stood out for the summer or used among seasonal displays. Take them in before the nights get cold.

Plant spring-flowering bulbs as soon as there are vacant containers.

Take cuttings of tender perennials if you have somewhere frost-free to overwinter them.

MID-AUTUMN

Plant spring-flowering bulbs as soon as possible.

Protect slightly tender shrubs and trees in cold areas (see *Late Autumn*). In most areas wait for another month. In mild to warm areas this is not a problem.

Plant bare-root plants, container-grown plants can be planted at any time.

LATE AUTUMN

Plant up some bulbs in plant pots to fill in gaps and bring pockets of interest in spring. The main spring bulb-planting season is finishing. Put them in half-pots unless the bulbs are very large, as the smaller rootball is easier to accommodate when infilling containers already planted. Keep the pots on a spare piece of ground and set them in position as they come into flower.

Protect containers that are not frostproof in cold areas by removing the compost and putting the empty containers in a dry place (perhaps a shed).

Protect slightly tender plants that are likely to be killed over winter in your area. The most tender must be taken indoors or into a conservatory, but many that are only likely to be killed by a severe winter, will survive outside with a little protection.

EARLY WINTER

Check containers, clean them if necessary, and make any repairs.

Check that winter protection is satisfactory and reposition any that has worked loose in autumn winds.

MID-WINTER

Check winter containers and pick off any dead or dying leaves.

Sow seasonal bedding plants that require a long growing season, such as zonal pelargoniums and fibrous-rooted begonias. If you do not have a greenhouse, buy plants in spring.

LATE WINTER

Sow summer annual plants if you have a warm protected area. Just a few plants can often be raised on a light window ledge indoors.

Check over winter and spring containers and remove any dead or dying flowers or foliage.

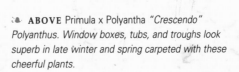

ABOVE Primula x Polyantha *"Crescendo" Polyanthus*. Window boxes, tubs, and troughs look superb in late winter and spring carpeted with these cheerful plants.

INDEX